THE USBORNE
LIVING WORLD
ENCYCLOPEDIA

Leslie Colvin and Emma Speare

Designed by Steve Page

Illustrated by
Isabel Bowring, Kuo Kang Chen,
Sandra Fernandez, Ian Jackson,
Steven Kirk, Rachel Lockwood
and Chris Shields

Additional designs by
John Russell, Sandy Wegener and Kathy Ward

Scientific advisors:
Steve Pollock and Ruth Taylor

Edited by Corinne Stockley
Editorial assistant: Fiona Patchett

Contents

4 The story of the Earth
6 Environments
8 Seasonal changes
10 Long-term changes
12 Cycles in nature
14 Plant life
16 Animal life
18 Extinctions

20 The seas and oceans
22 The ocean surface
24 Fish
26 The depths of the ocean
28 Coral reefs
30 Shorelines
32 Estuaries

34 Islands
36 Island life

38 Grasslands
40 Grassland plants
42 Grassland plant-eaters
44 Grassland meat-eaters
46 Survival on the grasslands
48 Life underground

50 Deserts
52 Coping with dryness
54 Coping with desert
   temperatures
56 Rain in the desert

58 Temperate forests
60 Deciduous forests
62 Up in the canopy
64 The forest floor
66 Northern evergreen
   forests
68 Winter in the northern
   forests
70 Australia's hot, dry forests

72 Polar regions
74 The Antarctic
76 The Arctic

78 Mountains
80 Living in a mountain climate
82 An isolated life

84 Rivers and lakes
86 Getting oxygen
   underwater
88 Fresh water plants and
   animals
90 Living by rivers and lakes
92 Water birds
94 The Amazon

96 Tropical rain forests
98 Rain forest plants
100 The rain forest floor
102 Climbing and gliding
104 Monkeys and apes
106 Rain forest hunters
108 Colors in the rain
    forest

110 Living with people
112 People and parasites

114 Endangered species
116 Describing living things
118 Glossary
121 Index

About this book

There are millions of different kinds of living things on Earth. Some are giant, such as blue whales and redwood trees, but others are very tiny, including many insects. All of them need food and shelter, which they get from their natural surroundings, or environment.

The first section of this book is about living things and their environments. The rest of the book groups together animals and plants by the environments where they are found. For example, squid and seaweeds are found in the seas and oceans, so they are in that section.

If you are not sure which section to find an animal or plant in, then look it up in the index (pages 121-128).

Some words have an asterisk*. This means they are explained somewhere else in the book. A footnote at the bottom of the page tells you where to look for the explanation. Difficult words are printed in **bold type** where they are mentioned and explained. There are lots of explanations of words in the glossary (pages 118-120).

This picture shows the Florida Everglades. Many different birds and fish live here as well as alligators and snakes.

The story of the Earth

The Earth is a spinning ball of hot, partly liquid rock, covered with a thin, outer crust. There are large cracks in the crust called plate boundaries, which divide into separate areas, called plates.

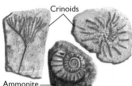

Crust

Plate

Plate boundary

The plates move

The partly liquid rock below the plates moves, making the plates themselves move about two centimeters (one inch) a year. They rub against each other as they move.

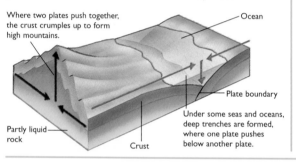

Where two plates push together, the crust crumples up to form high mountains.

Ocean

Plate boundary

Under some seas and oceans, deep trenches are formed, where one plate pushes below another plate.

Partly liquid rock

Crust

Fossils

Animals and plants that died a long time ago mostly rotted away. Sometimes, their hard parts, such as bones, were preserved in rocks as **fossils**.

Crinoids

Ammonite

Fossils show us what kinds of plants and animals lived as long time ago. Some, such as corals and crinoids, still live on Earth today, but many more, such as ammonites, died out. When all the members of one living thing have died out, it is extinct. For more about extinctions, see pages 18-19.

Life on Earth

When the Earth was formed, 4,600 million years ago, it was too hot for rain to fall. It was a very, very long time before the seas and oceans formed. ▼

3,500 million years ago, the ▲ first living things were alive in the oceans. They were too small to see, like the germs that make people ill today.

Simple animals, such as jellyfish and corals, and simple plants, such as algae, lived about 700 million years ago. ▼

400 million years ago, the ▲ first land plants grew on Earth. Fish and shelled animals lived in the seas.

4

Where animals and plants live today

Much of the Earth's land was once joined in one piece. As the plates moved, seas and mountains formed.

This stopped animals from moving over all the land and explains why living things are found in different places today.

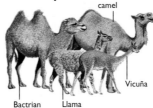

Arabian camel

Vicuña

Bactrian camel

Llama

There are lots of camel-like animals around the world. Their ancestors lived when the land was all one piece.

They became cut off from each other when the oceans formed. Over millions of years, each group developed differently.

Wombats are burrowing forest animals. They are slightly bigger than badgers.

The duck-billed platypus dives under water to hunt for food.

Tree kangaroos feed on fruit and leaves.

55 million years ago Australia broke away from Antarctica. Many animals, such as kangaroos, wombats and platypuses, exist only in Australia.

Some give birth to very tiny babies, which live in the mother's pouch for many weeks. The animals are marsupials*.

230 million years ago, dinosaurs were alive on Earth. They were land-living reptiles*. There were also flying reptiles and swimming reptiles.

65 million years ago, the dinosaurs died out (for more about why, see page 18). ▼

Apes, such as gorillas, are close relatives of humans. The earliest human fossils were found in Africa. They are two million years old. ▼

340 million years ago, insects and amphibians* lived in the swampy jungles which covered the land.

The first mammals* were small shrew-like animals which lived 225 million years ago.

The first apes lived 35 million years ago.

*This is a group of animals. For more about animal groups, see page 116.

5

Environments

The natural surroundings of an animal or plant are called its environment. There are many different environments around the world. They vary because of such things as temperature and different amounts of sunshine and rain.

The sections of this book from pages 20 to 113 look at the main environments of the world, such as tropical forests, deserts and oceans. All the plants and animals in these areas have become good at living in their particular environment.

Cacti store water in their systems, which helps them live in dry desert areas.

Polar bears have thick fur, which helps then to survive the icy, Arctic winters.

Changing environments

All environments have regular changes, such as the change between day and night, the changes in seasons and the movement of the tides on a seashore. Plants and animals are used to living with these changes. Other changes are more gradual, long-term changes (see pages 10-11).

Tidal changes

Animals that live on the seashore are used to living with the regular changes in the tides. There is more about this on pages 30-31.

When the tide comes back up the shore, they unfold and their tentacles wave around in the water.

Sea anemones pull their tentacles in when the tide is out, so that they do not dry up.

In the daytime

Many animals, from bears to bees, wake up when the sun comes up, live and feed all day and go to sleep at night. They are active during the day.

Wood sorrel

Bee

Many brightly colored flowers open during the day. Insects such as bees drink their nectar (see page 14).

At night

At night, plants cannot make food by photosynthesis, as there is no sunlight. They take in oxygen and give off moisture and carbon dioxide, just like animals do all the time.

The flowers and leaves of some plants close up when night comes.

Green plants make their food in the daytime, because they need sunlight to do it. They use the sun's energy to join water and carbon dioxide (a gas from the air) to make sugar. This is their food. As they do this they make another gas called oxygen, which they let out into the air. The whole process is called **photosynthesis.**

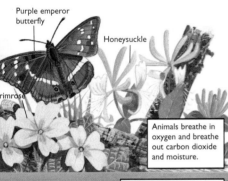

Purple emperor butterfly

Honeysuckle

Primrose

Animals breathe in oxygen and breathe out carbon dioxide and moisture.

Privet hawk moth

Some flowers stay open. Animals can detect their strong, sweet scent. Moths use feathery antennae to find flowers to feed from.

Stag beetle

Finding food at night

Many animals, such as moths, bats and foxes sleep in the day and are active at night. They are called **nocturnal** animals and often have special things about them that help them to hunt for food at night.

The gecko is a kind of lizard. It feeds on moths and insects at night. Like many nocturnal animals, it has large, sensitive eyes, which help it to see in very dim light.

Gecko

Many bats make very high-pitched squeaks to help them find their way at night.

Pipistrelle bat

Squeak sent out

Echoes bounce back

Bats listen for echoes as they squeak. Echoes happen when sound bounces off objects.

Bats find their way because they can tell from the echoes where obstacles are. Their large, sensitive ears help them detect different echoes, for example, echoes from trees they want to avoid, or from insects they want to catch.

Seasonal changes

Seasons are times of year with different conditions, such as weather and temperature. They change from one to the next in a yearly cycle. Around the world, plants and animals are good at dealing with the changes of seasons.

Seasons around the world

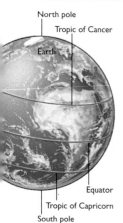

North pole
Tropic of Cancer
Earth
Equator
Tropic of Capricorn
South pole

Most places in the **tropics** (inside the imaginary tropic lines) are never very cold, and have two seasons - a wet, rainy season and a dry one. Near the equator (the middle imaginary line) it is hot and wet all year round.

Temperate areas (outside the tropic lines) have spring, summer, autumn and winter. Generally, the closer a place is to the north or south pole, the cooler its summers are the colder its winters.

The plant year

Green plants need sunlight and water to make food and grow. They grow most in spring and summer, or the wet season, and have different ways of surviving winter or the dry season.

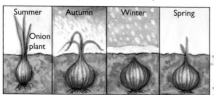

Summer | Autumn | Winter | Spring
Onion plant

Many plants have a resting stage. Some store up food in swollen parts of themselves under the ground. They die away above ground in the winter and rest until spring, when they grow new shoots. Carrots, onions and potatoes are all kinds of plant food stores that people eat.

The animal year

Many animals, such as reptiles*, can survive the cold or dry season by slowing down and becoming less active. When it gets warmer, or wetter, they go back to normal. Other animals cannot do this. They have other ways of surviving harsh seasons.

Many animals, such as dormice, sleep all winter. This is called **hibernation.** They feed and get fat all summer so they can sleep a long time without eating.

Most mammals* and birds produce their young in spring when there is more food about, so their young can get older and stronger before winter comes.

Deciduous trees, such as oak and beech, shed their leaves in autumn because there is not enough sunshine in the winter for their leaves to make food. They rest over winter and grow new leaves in spring from buds.

Beech tree

Bud

New leaf

The buds contain tiny leaves and shoots made the previous year.

*Mammals, Reptiles, 116.

Many birds and other animals make long journeys each year, called **migrations** (see page 42), to places where there is more food. For example, swallows nest in Europe in the spring. In autumn, they fly to Africa. They return in the spring when it is too dry in Africa.

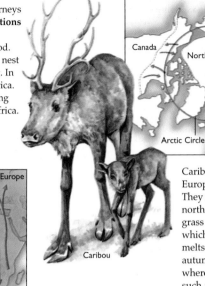
Caribou

Asia
Canada
North pole
Area where caribou herds migrate.
Arctic Circle
Europe

Europe
Swallows
Africa

Caribou (called reindeer in Europe and Asia) also migrate. They spend summer in the Arctic north. Huge herds feed on the grass and other small plants which grow quickly when the ice melts. They migrate south in the autumn, to evergreen forests where they feed on small plants such as lichens, under the snow.

Evergreen trees have leaves that last for several years and fall off gradually. They are never bare. For more about evergreen and deciduous trees, see pages 58-59.

Some evergreen trees, such as pine and fir, have long, thin leaves, called needles. Many of them grow quite far north, where summers are short and cool and winters freezing. By keeping their leaves all year, they can start growing fast as soon as spring arrives.

Needles
Pine tree

Desert flowers after rain

All deserts are very dry. Some years they may have no rain, other years they have a very short rainy season. The seeds of many desert plants only grow into new plants when enough rain falls. Then they flower and produce new seeds very fast. The seeds contain food stores.

9

Long-term changes

All the animals and plants in one area form a community. From year to year, the community does not change much, but over a long period it can change a great deal.

Food chains and webs

A **food chain** is a series of living things, linked together because each is the food for the next one. Green plants make their own food, so they start food chains. They are called **producers**. Animals cannot make their own food, so they must eat plants or other animals. They are called **consumers**. Animals can be first, second or third level consumers, depending on what kind of food they eat. **Food webs** link together different food chains in a community.

This is a diagram of a North American forest food web.

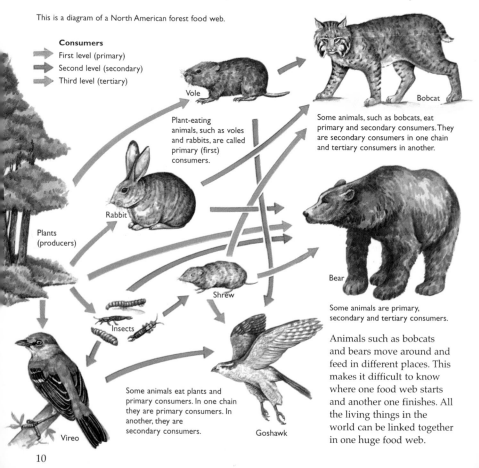

Consumers
→ First level (primary)
→ Second level (secondary)
→ Third level (tertiary)

Vole

Bobcat

Plant-eating animals, such as voles and rabbits, are called primary (first) consumers.

Some animals, such as bobcats, eat primary and secondary consumers. They are secondary consumers in one chain and tertiary consumers in another.

Rabbit

Plants (producers)

Shrew

Bear

Some animals are primary, secondary and tertiary consumers.

Insects

Some animals eat plants and primary consumers. In one chain they are primary consumers. In another, they are secondary consumers.

Vireo

Goshawk

Animals such as bobcats and bears move around and feed in different places. This makes it difficult to know where one food web starts and another one finishes. All the living things in the world can be linked together in one huge food web.

10

Changing communities

In a natural community the numbers of producers and consumers is balanced. There is enough food and the community does not change. It is stable.

However, the balance is easily upset. For example, if a disease kills all the primary consumers, this affects all the members of the food chain.

Secondary consumers die because there is not enough food.

Primary consumers die.

Plants grow better because they are being eaten less.

Big changes to a community set off a series of long term changes as nature tries to make it stable again.

For instance, after a forest fire the community is destroyed. Plants such as grass and ferns grow fast, covering the ground.

Small bushes grow and kill these plants by blocking their light. As new kinds of plants grow, different animals come to feed.

This type of slow change is called **succession**. After 200 years there may be a new community of forest plants and animals again.

When people clear areas for farming and keep them clear, they stop succession from happening. Natural communities are lost forever.

Regular changes

Natural changes in a community may follow a regular cycle. In the Arctic community, lemming numbers depend on the amount of food (plants) and the number of hunters, such as arctic foxes.

1. Lemmings live underground. They give birth to many young, which grow up quickly and give birth themselves, so their numbers can increase fast.

2. Lots of hungry lemmings means lots of food for the arctic foxes and so their numbers can increase too, but the plants suffer.

4. Fewer lemmings means that the plants can recover. Also, there is not enough food for the foxes, so many die and the cycle starts again.

3. Every few years there are so many lemmings that their food runs out. Most of them set off to look for new homes. Only a few stay behind.

Cycles in nature

All living things are made up of substances such as water, oxygen, nitrogen and carbon. They take them in from the environment, change them inside their bodies and use them to live and grow. When the living things die, and their bodies rot*, the substances go back to the environment. These substances are recycled, or used again and again, in nature.

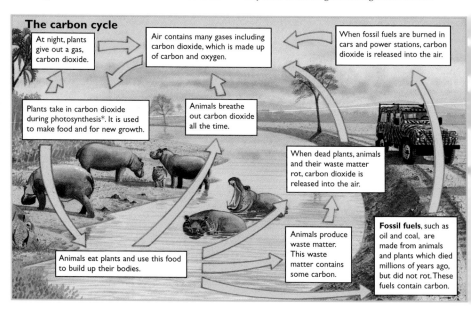

The carbon cycle

At night, plants give out a gas, carbon dioxide.

Air contains many gases including carbon dioxide, which is made up of carbon and oxygen.

When fossil fuels are burned in cars and power stations, carbon dioxide is released into the air.

Plants take in carbon dioxide during photosynthesis*. It is used to make food and for new growth.

Animals breathe out carbon dioxide all the time.

When dead plants, animals and their waste matter rot, carbon dioxide is released into the air.

Animals eat plants and use this food to build up their bodies.

Animals produce waste matter. This waste matter contains some carbon.

Fossil fuels, such as oil and coal, are made from animals and plants which died millions of years ago, but did not rot. These fuels contain carbon.

The greenhouse effect

Carbon dioxide in the air around the Earth keeps it warm, in the same way as glass in a greenhouse keeps everything inside it warm. This is called the **greenhouse effect**.

In a greenhouse, light from the sun goes through the glass, heating up everything inside.

This heat cannot get out again through the glass. More and more heat is trapped throughout the day.

Light from the sun goes through the glass.

The heat cannot get out again.

As light from the sun goes through the carbon dioxide and hits the Earth, much of the heat cannot get out.

Since people started burning fossil fuels, extra carbon dioxide has been released into the air. It may be building up.

If it does build up, the greenhouse effect may increase and the Earth may get warmer. The warming of the Earth is **global warming**.

12   *Photosynthesis, 7; Rot, 65.

Nitrogen in nature

Nitrogen is a gas in the air. Tiny living things called bacteria* change it into substances called **nitrates**, which all other living things need. It is then recycled in nature.

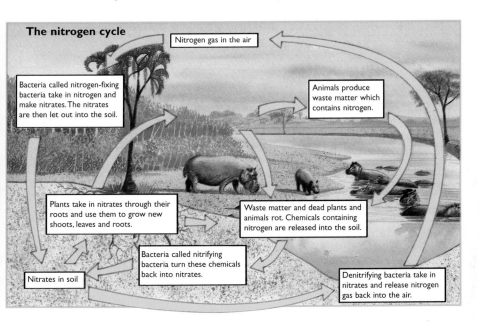

The nitrogen cycle

Nitrogen gas in the air

Bacteria called nitrogen-fixing bacteria take in nitrogen and make nitrates. The nitrates are then let out into the soil.

Animals produce waste matter which contains nitrogen.

Plants take in nitrates through their roots and use them to grow new shoots, leaves and roots.

Waste matter and dead plants and animals rot. Chemicals containing nitrogen are released into the soil.

Bacteria called nitrifying bacteria turn these chemicals back into nitrates.

Nitrates in soil

Denitrifying bacteria take in nitrates and release nitrogen gas back into the air.

Farming

Farming upsets the nitrogen cycle, because crop plants, such as wheat, which take in nitrates from the soil, are cut and taken away to be sold.

Farmers must replace the nitrates, so that they can grow more crop plants in the same field the following year.

Many modern farmers do this by putting chemical fertilizers, which contain nitrates, on their fields.

It is difficult to judge how much fertilizer is needed. If too much is added, the extra nitrates are washed out of the soil, by rain, into rivers.

This pollutes the rivers, lakes and seas, killing many plants, fish and other animals (for more about this, see page 87).

*Bacteria 113

13

Plant life

All living things produce new life, or reproduce. Most plants do this by growing flowers, which make seeds. (For more about other plants, see pages 116-117.)

The seeds then grow into new plants. The changes from seed to plant to flower to seed happen again and again in a natural cycle.

From seed to plant

Seeds contain a food store. They need this for energy to grow the first root, shoot and leaves. This first growth is a **germination**.

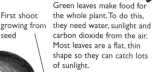

First shoot growing from seed

First root

Green leaves make food for the whole plant. To do this, they need water, sunlight and carbon dioxide from the air. Most leaves are a flat, thin shape so they can catch lots of sunlight.

Branching roots go deep into the soil. They take in simple substances, such as nitrates*, other minerals and water, that the plant needs.

Shoot

Seed

Inside the shoots, roots and leaves of land plants there are two kinds of tubes. These carry water and food around the plant. Xylem tubes carry water from the roots up to the leaves. Phloem tubes carry food from the leaves to other parts of the plant.

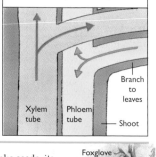

Branch to leaves

Xylem tube

Phloem tube

Shoot

Flowers

Most flowers grow at special times of the year. They make new seeds.

Flowers have male parts and female parts. Some plants have both in the same flower, some have only male parts in one kind of flower and female parts in another kind of flower.

Apple blossom

Anthers are the male parts of the flower. They make many tiny pollen grains.

The female part of the flower is the ovary. This makes "eggs" called ovules.

This flower has been cut in half.

Wild rose

For a flower to make seeds, its ovules need to join up with pollen grains. This is called **pollination**. Plants do this in different ways.

Plants such as grasses have dull colored flowers. They make light pollen which is carried by the wind. The flowers are pollinated if pollen from a flower of the same kind lands on them.

Foxglove

Daisy

Plants with brightly colored flowers make a sweet liquid, called nectar. As insects drink this, they touch the anthers and pollen sticks to them. If they carry pollen to another flower of the same kind, it is pollinated.

After pollination, the ovules form new seeds, which the plant scatters. If they land in places where conditions are right, they start to grow. Different plants scatter their seeds in different ways (see pages 34-35).

14   *Nitrates, 13.

Growth

Plants grow faster at different times. In temperate areas they grow most in spring and summer, in the tropics they grow best whenever there is enough rain.

Many small plants live for one growing season, then they make seeds and die.

Other plants, such as trees and shrubs grow for many years. They produce new seeds each year.

Sunflower

Cypress tree

Poppy

Pansy

Trees

All trees grow new leaves and flowers each year.

Some trees, such as fruit trees, have large, bright flowers (their pollen is often carried by insects).

Trees such as the oak have small, dull flowers (their pollen is carried by the wind to other oak trees).

A tree's trunk grows thicker and stronger each year as the tree grows larger.

Tough bark covers the trunk and branches. It protects the layer of delicate phloem inside.

Inside the phloem, rings of xylem, called **annual rings**, make up the wood. These show the age of the tree because each ring is one year's growth.

The oldest xylem is in the middle.

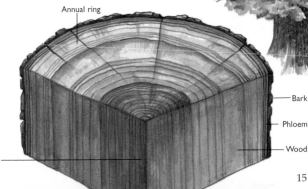

Annual ring

Bark

Phloem

Wood

Animal life

Like plants, all animals reproduce (produce new life). Their young grow up and produce new young animals themselves. This happens again and again in a natural cycle. Different animals do this in slightly different ways. Producing young animals is called breeding.

Babies

Most animals lay eggs, and the babies hatch out from them. But one group of animals, called **mammals*** give birth to babies (up to ten at a time). The parents care for their babies until they have grown up and can look after themselves. Some babies, such as cats, dogs, mice and rats, are born blind and helpless. Their mother makes a nest for them and keeps them warm and clean.

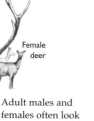

Male deer

Female deer

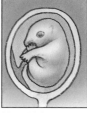

All mammal babies feed on milk from their mother's body.

Adult males and females often look different from each other. For example, male deer grow antlers on their head. Female deer never grow antlers.

There are also differences inside their bodies. These differences allow them to breed, or have babies of their own.

Some babies, such as horses, stay inside their mother until they are quite large. Soon after they are born they can stand and are on their feet, running with their mother.

Tiny sperm are produced by males.

Large eggs are produced by females.

For a new animal life to be produced, a single sperm must join together with, or **fertilize**, an egg. This happens differently in different animals.

Mammal baby growing inside its mother.

Lions mating

Male mammals and some other male animals, push their sperm into the female's body. This is called **mating**.

In mammals, the fertilized eggs grow into babies inside the female's body, and then the babies are born.

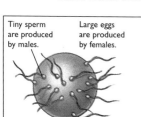

16   *Mammals, 116.

Egg layers

Most animals, apart from mammals, lay eggs. Some of them mate and lay fertilized eggs. Others shed their sperm and eggs in water and the eggs are fertilized as they mix with the sperm. Babies hatch out of both kinds of eggs.

Female ostriches lay fertilized eggs.

Changes

Many animals' eggs hatch into young that look very different from the adults. The young are called **larvae**. Different larvae change in different ways, until they become adults.

Animals, such as frogs live on land, but go to ponds and lakes to lay hundreds of soft eggs in the water.

Frog larvae, called tadpoles, look very different from their parents. They have a tail for swimming.

Most tadpoles are caught and eaten. A few survive long enough to lose their tails slowly and grow legs.

When they are frogs, they leave the water. The next year they come back to lay their own eggs.

Frogs are threatened by pollution in ponds and rivers because they need clean water for their young to develop.

Fast or slow

Different kinds of animals produce different numbers of young, which take different amounts of time to grow up.

Mice

Animals such as mice have lots of babies and give birth many times each year. Their babies grow up quickly and have babies of their own. They are called **fast breeders.**

Animals such as rhinos are **slow breeders.** They have one baby every few years. After several more years it is grown up and can have babies itself.

Rhinoceros

Many endangered species*, such as some tropical butterflies and whales, are slow breeders. This means that if a natural disaster, or too much hunting, kills lots of them they take many years to increase in number again.

Extinctions

A particular kind of plant or animal, such as star cacti or koalas, is called a species. If the last one dies, that species is extinct. There are none left to produce new young ones. Extinctions have happened slowly and naturally throughout the history of life on Earth. But today huge numbers of species are in danger of dying out quickly. They are called endangered species.

In the past

In the past, species died out because of natural changes, such as changes in the Earth's surface or in the weather. New species filled the gaps left by the extinct ones, as nature tried to find a new balance (see page 11).

Dinosaurs

Woolly mammoth

65 million years ago the dinosaurs died out. No one really knows why, but some people think the climate became much colder after a huge rock called a meteor crash landed on Earth.

Mammals* such as woolly mammoths could live in a very cold climate. Over thousands of years new animals such as these filled the gaps left by the extinct dinosaurs.

The people problem

The number of people in the world gets bigger every year. By the year 2050 there may be 14 billion. People need food and homes. They clear large areas of wild land to use for farming and building.

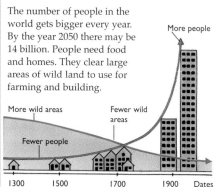

More people

More wild areas

Fewer wild areas

Fewer people

1300   1500   1700   1900   Dates

Why are species endangered?

Endangered species are those whose numbers are now very low. In the case of animals, they are usually slow breeders* and only just produce enough young to replace those that die. Different species of plants and animals are threatened for different reasons.

Many large animals, such as elephants, whales, gorillas, alligators and tigers are hunted for their tusks, skins and meat.

*Mammals, Reptiles, 116; Slow breeders, 17.

Many plants, such as cacti, and animals, such as butterflies, birds and monkeys, are taken from the wild and sold abroad to collectors. Some animals are sold as pets to zoos.

Philippine eagle

Spider monkey

Swallowtail butterfly

Galapagos giant tortoises cannot compete with animals such as rabbits, that eat their food. The rabbits were brought to the islands when people came to live there.

Giant tortoise

Giant pandas are rare animals. In the past many died when the forests where they lived were cleared to make farmland. A disease could make the few that remain die out.

For more about endangered species, see pages 114-115.

Giant panda

Why does it matter?

Not only do we find plants and animals beautiful to look at, but we would also all die without them. Plants and animals are important to people for many different reasons.

Plants and animals recycle all the natural substances needed for life (see pages 12-13).

Wood from trees is used for building, making paper and as a fuel.

In the past, people tamed wild animals, such as wild cattle, goats and pigs and kept them for their milk, skins and meat.

Drinks such as tea, coffee and cocoa and many herbs, spices, oils and medicines come from plants.

Tamed animals are best at surviving in the areas they come from. For example, in Africa, cows from Europe often die of diseases. Today Africans are trying to farm native animals, such as the eland.

If people manage to protect endangered species today, by preserving the wild areas where they live, then in the future they may help people solve world problems. For example, not long ago people discovered that a tree, called the Moreton Bay chestnut, makes a chemical that may help treat the disease AIDS.

19

The seas and oceans

Most of the Earth is covered by seas or oceans. There are five great oceans and many smaller seas. The water in them is not like tap water. Instead it is a salty soup full of millions of very tiny floating plants and animals called plankton (see pages 22-23).

These are views from different sides of the Earth. They show that the Pacific Ocean covers nearly half the Earth.

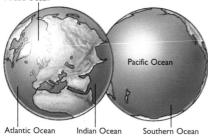

Arctic Ocean

Pacific Ocean

Atlantic Ocean   Indian Ocean   Southern Ocean

The water cycle

All living things need water. The water on Earth is used over and over again.

1. The sun heats up the land and the surface of rivers, lakes and the sea. This makes some of this water turn into water vapor, which rises into the air.

2. As water vapor rises, it cools, turning back into water droplets. These form clouds.

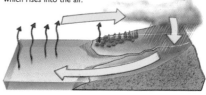

4. Any water not taken in by plants or the soil joins up with rivers. All the rivers flow back to the sea.

3. As the clouds get colder, the droplets get bigger or turn into ice crystals. They then fall as rain, snow or hail.

Different parts of the oceans

The temperature of the oceans and the amount and kinds of minerals in them varies in different parts, at different depths and at different times of the year.

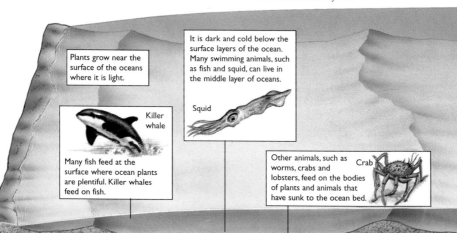

Plants grow near the surface of the oceans where it is light.

It is dark and cold below the surface layers of the ocean. Many swimming animals, such as fish and squid, can live in the middle layer of oceans.

Killer whale

Squid

Many fish feed at the surface where ocean plants are plentiful. Killer whales feed on fish.

Other animals, such as worms, crabs and lobsters, feed on the bodies of plants and animals that have sunk to the ocean bed.

Crab

Important plants

Ocean plants, including plant plankton, make their own food by photosynthesis* using sunlight. Without these plants there would be no food or fish or other ocean animals.

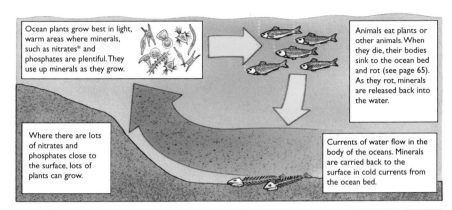

Ocean plants grow best in light, warm areas where minerals, such as nitrates* and phosphates are plentiful. They use up minerals as they grow.

Animals eat plants or other animals. When they die, their bodies sink to the ocean bed and rot (see page 65). As they rot, minerals are released back into the water.

Where there are lots of nitrates and phosphates close to the surface, lots of plants can grow.

Currents of water flow in the body of the oceans. Minerals are carried back to the surface in cold currents from the ocean bed.

In the middle of the ocean there are trenches up to 11km (seven miles) deep and underwater mountains taller than any found on land.

Huge flocks of sea birds feed on the many fish that live in the shallow oceans near land.

Sea birds

Rivers flow into the sea bringing extra minerals, washed from the soil and rocks on land.

Close to the continents the ocean bed rises up to meet the land. This part of it is called the **continental shelf.** The seas or oceans above it are more shallow.

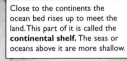

Worm

Peculiar fish and worms live in the deep, dark, freezing depths of the trenches.

Coral reefs grow in warm, clear, shallow water near the tropics. They provide food and shelter for thousands of different kinds of animals.

The ocean surface

Sunlight only reaches down about 100m (1,300ft) below the surface of the sea. Plants need the sun's energy to make their food, so this top layer is the only place ocean plants can live. Many animals also live and feed in this top layer.

Plankton

The very tiny plants and animals that float in the top layer of the oceans are called **plankton**. The plants are called phytoplankton, the animals zooplankton. Phytoplankton are the basis of all life in the oceans. They are food for small animals who in turn are eaten by larger ones. Phytoplankton are often amazing shapes. Like all plants, they can make their own food by photosynthesis*. They get substances such as carbon dioxide and minerals from the sea water.

Phytoplankton

Zooplankton

Zooplankton swim near the surface at night, eating the phytoplankton. During the day they sink deeper to hide where it is darker.

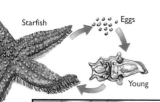

Starfish

Eggs

Young

Many animals, such as starfish, lay thousands of eggs. Their young hatch out and feed off the plankton. Most of them die before they can lay eggs themselves, but a few survive.

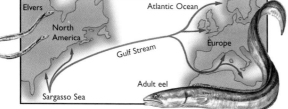

Elvers

North America

Atlantic Ocean

Europe

Gulf Stream

Adult eel

Sargasso Sea

Eels lay eggs in the Sargasso Sea. Their young float to Europe in the Gulf Stream current. Slowly they become elvers (young eels) and swim up rivers. 12 years later they are adults and swim back to the same sea to lay their eggs.

Plankton eaters

Many sea creatures feed on plankton. They sieve it out of the water using special parts of themselves. This is called **filter feeding**.

These creatures spend most of their time near the surface, where the plankton is.

Baleen whales push water out of their mouth with their huge tongue.

Blue whale

Lots of animals, such as barnacles and other shelled animals, fix themselves in one place. Barnacles often choose a large object such as a ship or a whale.

Barnacles' bristly "arms" filter out plankton from the water.

There are two main kinds of whale. Blue whales belong to the kind called **baleen whales**. The other kind are toothed whales*. Baleen whales gulp mouthfuls of plankton-rich seawater. As they push it out again, horny sheets called **baleen plates** filter out tiny animals called krill.

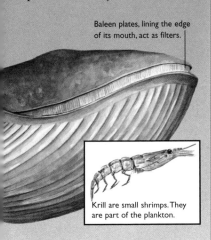

Baleen plates, lining the edge of its mouth, act as filters.

Krill are small shrimps. They are part of the plankton.

Many fish of all sizes, from huge whale sharks to tiny anchovies, have fine bones called gill rakers attached to their gills (their breathing parts). These filter food, such as plankton, out of the water as the fishes "breathe" (for more about how gills work, see page 86).

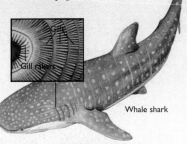

Gills

Gill rakers

Whale shark

Other surface animals

Many other animals spend most of their lives near the ocean surface. They do this for different reasons.

Dolphin

Like all whales, dolphins developed from land-living animals and still breathe air. They swim near the surface, leaping high out of the water.

Sea snake

Sea snakes have the deadliest poison of all snakes. They breathe air (their ancestors were land snakes). They swim by pushing their bodies in and out of an S shape.

Leatherback

Turtles have flippers and a flat shell to help them swim. They also breathe air. The leatherback is the largest kind. It can grow to be twice as heavy as a polar bear.

Portuguese man o'war

Float

The Portuguese man o'war is really a huge group of jellyfish all joined together. It gets bigger by growing new baby jellyfish that stay attached to it. It has stinging tentacles up to 20m (66ft) long and uses its gas-filled float like a sail as it drifts over the surface.

*Toothed whales, 27.

Fish

The first fish lived 400 million years ago. Today, about 200,000 different kinds of fish live in every part of the seas and oceans. They are all superb swimmers.

Swimming

Water is much harder to move through than air. Most fish have bodies that are a smooth shape to help them swim.

Most fish swim by beating their tail fins from side to side.

Tail fin

Tail

Fish turn from side to side using the fins which stick out from the bottom and top of their bodies.

They move up or down in the water using the fins on each side of their body.

Some fish can twist these side fins. They use them as brakes. For more about fins see page 119.

Lots of fish have a "bag" of air, called a **swim bladder**, inside their bodies. This makes them lighter for their size so that they can stop swimming and just float in the water.

Sharks stay up in the water because of the water moving over their fins.

Position of swim bladder

Other fish have side fins fixed in one position. Water moving over their fins keeps them up in the water, in the same way as air moving over airplane wings keeps planes up in the air.

If they stop swimming they sink. Also, they have no "brakes", so they cannot stop quickly.

Body shapes

Different kinds of fish look very different. Some of them are sleek, fast swimming hunters that travel long distances each year. Other flatter or fatter fish spend all their life in one small area of rocky shore, ocean bed or coral reef.

Great white shark

Flying fish are small fast-swimming fish. They do not actually fly. But, to escape attackers, they leap out of the water and glide using their large side fins.

Flying fish

Plaice live close to the sea bed and are flat fish. They can hide by changing color to blend in with the sea bed. When plaice first hatch they look like normal fish. After a few days one eye has moved over the top of their heads. They swim on their sides.

Plaice

Great white sharks are huge hunting fish. They have an amazing sense of smell which they use to find their food, and many rows of sharp, backward-pointing teeth.

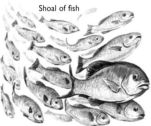

Sail fish are large hunters. Their sleek shape helps them to swim faster than any other fish, at over 100kph (60mph).

Sail fish

Rays are flat fish. They swim using their huge side fins. The manta ray is the biggest ray in the world, but it only eats plankton*.

Ray

Remora

The remora uses its back fin as a sucker to "hitch rides" on other animals. It does not harm them, but in this way it can travel long distances.

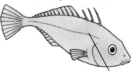

The remora's back fin works as a sucker.

Living in groups

Many small fish, such as damsel fish, swim in groups called **shoals**. They do this for protection from hunters. One fish on its own is easily caught and eaten, but a group may look like a big animal and confuse an attacker.

Shoal of fish

Most fish have sense organs, called **lateral lines**, that detect tiny movements in the water. They use them to sense other objects, including hunters, food and other members of the shoal. They also use them to find their way around.

Fish have one lateral line on each side of their body.

Each line is made up of a tube under the skin, with holes that come through from the skin.

Movements in the water around the fish make water in the tube move. The fish can sense these movements.

Lateral line

Holes Tube
Skin

*Plankton, 22.

25

The depths of the ocean

It is cold, dark and still in the depths of the ocean. No plants can grow, so animals eat other animals or dead plants and animals that sink slowly from the surface. Most animals in the ocean depths are small, often less than 30cm (12in) long. They are good at living in their strange world.

Big eaters, strange lights

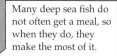

Many deep sea fish do not often get a meal, so when they do, they make the most of it.

The gulper eel can open its large mouth very wide and has a stretchy stomach. This means it can eat things bigger than itself.

Many creatures of the deep, such as hatchet fish, can produce blue-green light from special parts of their bodies. People say they are **luminous**.

Some deep sea fish, such as viper fish, use their luminous patches to help them find a mate in the pitch darkness.

Some angler fish use light to fish for food (smaller fish). They have one very long fin with a tip which produces light. The fish dangles this over its head and eats any small fish that come too close.

Deep sea hunters

Squid and octopuses are closely related and are both hunting animals, but they live quite different lives.

Squid are fast-swimming animals. They have eight short arms and two long ones, all with claws or suckers on them.

Deep-sea species have luminous patches on their skin. The largest kind, the giant squid, grows up to 14m (46ft) long.

Squid grab their prey with their long arms. They pull it close enough for their short arms to hold it firmly while they eat.

Squid have suckers on their tentacles to grip with.

Hiding in the dark

Many deep-sea animals, such as shrimps, are a red color. This looks black in blue-green light, so they are hidden from hunters in the dark.

Squid and octopuses have very good eyesight. They need to see well to hunt.

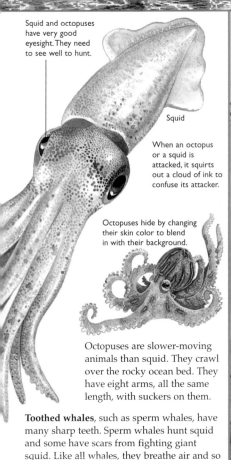

Squid

When an octopus or a squid is attacked, it squirts out a cloud of ink to confuse its attacker.

Octopuses hide by changing their skin color to blend in with their background.

Octopuses are slower-moving animals than squid. They crawl over the rocky ocean bed. They have eight arms, all the same length, with suckers on them.

Toothed whales, such as sperm whales, have many sharp teeth. Sperm whales hunt squid and some have scars from fighting giant squid. Like all whales, they breathe air and so live near the surface, but they can dive down very deep to find their food.

Sperm whale

The ocean bed

The ocean bed at the bottom of trenches can be over ten kilometers (six miles) below the surface. The mud on the sea bed is firm because it has been squashed by the weight of the water above.

Lobsters are related to crabs. They can swim, but usually walk over the ocean bed, looking for plants and animals to eat. Some lobsters travel very long distances this way.

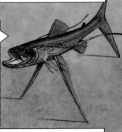

Tripod fish live close to the ocean bed. three of their fins have an extra long piece on the end, with a sensing tip. They use these to probe the muddy ocean bed for worms to eat.

Most sea spiders eat tiny animals, such as sea anemones. The deep-sea species include the largest spider of all, which can be up to about 75cm (30in) across.

Some kinds of giant tube worms live at the very bottom of the deep ocean trenches. They feed on bacteria* (tiny living things) which live around underwater volcanoes nearby.

*Bacteria, 113.

27

Coral reefs

Coral reefs are only found in warm, clear, salty water where there is lots of light. They were built by millions of tiny animals, over thousands of years. They are still being built today. Thousands of other animals live in and around them.

Reef builders

The animals that build reefs, called coral polyps, are like tiny sea anemones. Each one grows its own chalky skeleton. The body of the reef is made up of the skeletons of old polyps that have died: only the outermost layer is alive.

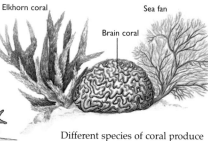

Elkhorn coral

Brain coral

Sea fan

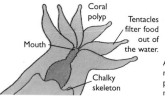

Coral polyp

Tentacles filter food out of the water.

Mouth

Chalky skeleton

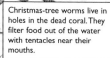

A coral polyp reproduces (produces new life) by growing a new baby polyp, called a **bud**, out of itself. Each new polyp grows its own skeleton.

Different species of coral produce buds in different ways. This gives each species its special shape, which builds up slowly. A reef is made of many different species.

Coral-reef animals

Many filter feeding* animals, such as barnacles, clams, fan worms and sponges, shelter in a reef and many fish swim gently around it. Coral reef fish are often special shapes or bright colors.

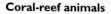

Sea horses are a type of fish. They swim upright in the water. The male sea horse looks after the eggs after he has fertilized* them. He keeps them in his pouch until they hatch into baby sea horses.

Christmas-tree worms live in holes in the dead coral. They filter food out of the water with tentacles near their mouths.

The crown of thorns starfish eats coral by sucking the polyps out of their shells.

Butterfly fish have stiff, straight snouts which they use to reach the coral polyps they feed on.

Giant clams grow up to one meter (three feet) long and lie buried in the reef, feeding. They use gills inside their shells to take oxygen from the water and also to sieve bits of food.

Sea urchins are hard and spiky. Their spikes are used for defense and moving around. Their mouths are underneath, so they "sit" on their food. Coral-reef species feed on tiny plants growing on the coral.

Reefs in danger

Coral reefs grow very slowly. Many of them are destroyed when the coral is sold to tourists or when bits of coral are used for building.

Island

Coral reef growing in shallow water

Reefs are built up by the living polyps on the outermost surface. They need lots of light to do this and grow very slowly. Damage to the reef in shallow water can be mended if new polyps spread to the damaged parts. But in deep water it is too dark for the polyps, so the reef dies.

Surgeon fish have a sharp bony blade poking out of the skin near their tails. They slash out with their tails when they feel threatened.

When attacked, puffer fish gulp water and swell up like a balloon. Many have spiky scales which stand out like needles when they swell up. One species, called the death puffer, is the most poisonous fish in the world.

Moray eels are hunting fish. They can grow up to three meters (ten feet) long. They have very thin bodies and hide in deep holes in the reef.

Living together

Some animals around coral reefs live with, or on, other animals. By doing this they usually get food more easily or gain protection.

The hermit crab has no shell of its own, so it lives inside old sea shells. On coral reefs, sea anemones often share a hermit crab's shell home.

Sea anemone

The sea anemone, with its stinging tentacles, protects them both. The crab leaves plenty of food scraps which the anemone can eat.

Hermit crab

Sea cucumber

The pearl fish is long and thin. It lives in an animal called a sea cucumber. It feeds on the insides of the cucumber, but the cucumber is not harmed, because it grows back as fast as the pearl fish eats it.

Pearl fish

Cleaner wrasse

Fish called cleaner wrasse clean many bigger fish by eating the small animal pests which live on them. They even swim right inside their mouths to feed. The big fish know not to eat the cleaner fish because they make special movements as signals.

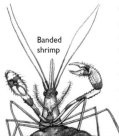

Banded shrimp

The banded, or cleaner, shrimp also cleans other coral reef animals of their pests. It waves its legs and antennae so that the animals know not to eat it.

29

Shorelines

Shorelines are the areas where the sea meets the land. They can be rocky cliffs, pebble or sandy beaches, mud flats* or a mixture or these. Waves wear away cliffs and move rocks around on beaches. Rocks are slowly worn into smooth pebbles and then into finer sand, which can be carried in sea water and washed up on other shores. Mud flats often form near estuaries*.

The tides

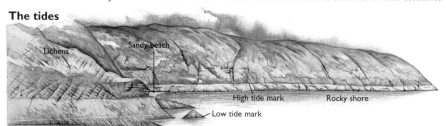

Lichens

Sandy beach

High tide mark

Rocky shore

Low tide mark

Twice a day the sea comes up the shore and then goes back. These sea movements are the **tides**. All sea creatures living on shores are exposed to the sun and the wind at low tide. If they dry out before the high tide covers them, they die.

Many animals live in bands along the shore. Shelled animals can live higher up, where they are uncovered most of the time. Starfish and worms live lower down the shore, where they are uncovered for less of the time.

Living with the tides

Seashore animals can survive even though waves batter the rocks and move the sand and pebbles around. They do this in different ways.

Some animals attach themselves to rocks. Others hide in cracks, or in rock pools which form at low tide. Some burrow under the shifting sand.

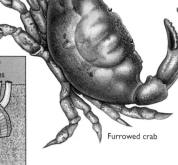

Furrowed crab

Animals such as mussels clean pollution out of the water. As they feed, they fill up with poisonous chemicals and harmful bacteria*. Other animals that eat them, however, are often poisoned.

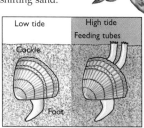

Low tide

High tide

Feeding tubes

Cockle

Foot

Mussels spend all their lives in one place, attached to rocks. When the tide goes out, they clamp their shells shut. This keeps some water inside and stops them from drying out.

Cockles live under the sand or mud, where it is damp. They have a "foot" for burrowing and two feeding tubes which reach up to the sea. These are pulled in at low tide.

Crabs eat the rotting bodies of dead animals and plants on the seashore. They burrow under the ground at low tide, or live in the sea, so they do not dry out in the air.

*Bacteria, 113; Estuaries, Mud flats, 32.

Oil pollution

In many places shorelines are now filthy and poisoned because of oil spilled from tankers, pipelines and oil rigs.

Any small living thing that gets covered in oil will die and so will animals, such as fish, which eat them. Oil also kills sea birds by destroying the waterproofing layer covering their feathers.

Some oil pollution in the sea comes from people who pour oil down drains, for example, after they have changed the oil in their car engines.

Dog whelks are hunters. They eat other shelled animals. First the whelk climbs onto the animal and drills a hole in its shell. Then it sucks out the soft parts of the animal.

Dog whelk

Starfish have five arms with rows of very powerful suckers on them. They can pull open a tightly shut shell and eat the animal inside.

Starfish

Shore birds

Wading birds, such as curlews, oystercatchers and knots, are common on sandy or muddy shores. Many come to breed at certain times of the year. Others stop for a rest during their migrations*.

Knots have a short beak and feed on shallow burrowing animals, such as crabs, shrimps and worms.

Curlews have a long, curved beak with a sensitive tip. They probe in mud or sand, seeking small worms or shelled animals, deep underground.

Oystercatchers have a long, straight beak. They feed on shelled animals, such as cockles and mussels, by splitting the shells open with their beak.

Seaweeds

Seaweeds are red, brown or green and feel slimy. They get substances that they need to grow, such as minerals, from the sea. They anchor themselves to rocks near the shore, with a part called a **holdfast** and make food by photosynthesis*, in their leaf-like branches, called **fronds.**

Like all plants, seaweeds need light to make their food. They can only grow in shallow areas where sea water holds them up near the ocean surface.

Fronds

Holdfast

Sea lettuce is a small, green seaweed. At low tide, it lies flat on the rocks. It has a slimy surface which stops it from drying out.

American giant kelp is a brown seaweed which grows off the coast of America. Its fronds grow to 100m (320ft) long. Bags of gas, called **bladders**, keep the fronds up in the water.

*Migrations, 9; Photosynthesis, 7.

Estuaries

Where a river enters the sea, the tide still comes in and goes out twice a day. When it comes in, it floods the river with salty water. Often the river then overflows and floods the nearby land with a mixture of salt water and fresh river water. The flooded part of the river is the estuary. When the tide goes out, the flood water goes too. The river still flows to the sea.

How estuaries form

Most estuaries are muddy places. Rivers carry **silt** with them. Silt is a mixture of very tiny pieces of rock and plant material. Near the sea, the river flows very slowly and the silt sinks to the bottom.

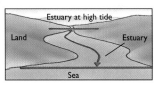

Estuary at high tide
Land
Estuary
Sea

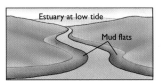

Estuary at low tide
Mud flats

The tide brings in sand and pebbles which mix with the silt, forming mud. When the tide goes out, the mud is left behind in the estuary. Slowly, large muddy areas, called **mud flats**, are built up.

Life in an estuary

Very few living things can survive in both fresh and salt water. But an estuary is home to vast numbers of those that can. They live with big changes in the saltiness of the water.

Plants such as cord grass and eel grass can grow on mud flats that flood, close to the river. Their roots trap the mud and stop it from being moved by the tides.

Eel grass

The mud flats farther away flood less often. Plants such as thrift and sea aster, which are less good at surviving changes in saltiness, grow here between the grasses.

Sea aster

The mud flats farthest from the river are rarely flooded. Many kinds of plants grow on them. The mud below is still quite soft, so these are marshy areas.

Mud flats are made of fine particles with only a few air spaces between them, unlike soil. Roots cannot grow down deep where there is no air, so most mud flat plants are small.

Some fish, such as salmon and eels, can live in both fresh and salt water.

Salmon lay their eggs up near the source (beginning) of rivers. When the young hatch, they swim down river and off into the ocean, where they live and feed for up to six years. Then they return up the same river to lay their eggs.

Salmon

Each river has a special "taste". This is how salmon tell which river they were hatched in.

Many tiny, shelled animals, such as spire shells and shrimps, live in the mud. 50,000 have been counted in a bucketful of mud.

Ragworms are related to earthworms. They live in estuaries and on muddy sea shores. They feed on the tiny animals in the mud.

Mangrove swamps

Sea at high tide

Sea at low tide

Prop roots

The roots growing out and down from the trunk are **prop roots**. They trap silt and support the tree.

Closely-packed mangrove trees often grow on the mud flats in the tropics, forming dense, swampy forests. These are called mangrove swamps. Like all estuary plants, mangrove trees cannot grow deep roots, as there is not enough air in the mud. They have roots that grow out and down from the trunk, or loop up out of the mud. This means they are above the water at low tide. The roots have patches on them that can take in the gas oxygen from the air.

Strange animals

Some odd fish live in mangrove swamps. The mudskipper crawls around on its stiff fins. It can leap by flicking itself into the air with its strong tail.

Mudskipper

Four-eyed fish

The four-eyed fish only has two eyes, but each is split into two halves. The top parts can see in air, the bottom parts in water, so it can see both above and below water at the same time.

Many kinds of crab, such as the fiddler crab, live on the muddy edges of the swamps. The male has one very large claw that it waves in the air to attract females or threaten other males.

Manatees have a split top lip that they use to pick up their food (plants).

There are two types of sea cow, the dugong and the manatee. Both can grow up to four meters (13ft) long. A third kind, Steller's sea cow, lived in the north Pacific, but is now extinct.

Archer fish can spit water into the air to knock insects off the underside of leaves.

Archer fish

Proboscis monkeys feed on the leaves and shoots of mangrove trees. They spend most of their time in the trees, although they are good swimmers.

Male proboscis monkeys make a honking noise to warn of danger. Their large noses may help them make a loud noise.

Islands

Islands vary in size from tiny coral islands, with no name, to Australia, a huge continent. Animals and plants on islands are separated by water from those on the mainland. People say island plants and animals are isolated from other plants and animals elsewhere.

How are islands formed?

Islands are formed in two main ways. The first is when land separates from the mainland. For example, Madagascar and New Zealand formed in this way over 20 million years ago. They had plants and animals on them from the start.

Mainland   New island with life on it.

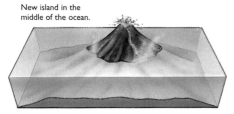
New island in the middle of the ocean.

The other way islands form is when volcanoes on the sea bed push up so much new rock that new land forms in the ocean. This is how the Galapagos and Hawaiian islands were formed, for example. Such volcanic islands have no life on them to start with.

New islands

Most new islands are volcanic islands. Once the volcano has stopped erupting, they are just lumps of bare rock. Gradually soil develops, plants grow and animals come to live on them.

Once there is soil on a new island, plants can grow. Plants spread by producing seeds. These are carried to islands by wind or water, or by birds and other animals.

Winds and ocean waves wear away the surface of the rocks into very tiny pieces. This process is called **erosion**.

Some plants, such as orchids, have seeds that are so light they can be carried by the wind.
Flower
Powdery seeds

Animals that feed in the sea, such as sea birds, seals and sea lions, are the first to arrive. They come to breed where there are no predators (hunting animals).

Their droppings rot slowly, mixing with the rock particles to form soil.

Others, such as thistles, have heavier seeds with feathery parachutes which catch the wind.

Coconuts are the seeds of palm trees. Their shells are waterproof. They float and can be carried by the sea.

Island visitors

Sea birds spend most of their lives at sea, feeding on fish. They come to islands in the middle of the ocean to nest, where there are few predators to threaten their young.

Albatross

Frigate birds have large wings and small legs. They attack other sea birds to make them vomit their food. Then they dive, catch the food and eat it.

Frigate Bird

Puffins make a nest by scraping a hole out of the cliffs. The colors on the male's beak only last while he tries to attract a mate.

Puffin

The albatross has the largest wing span of all. One kind, the wandering albatross, spends most of its time in the air. It feeds near Australia but nests on islands in the South Atlantic.

Blue-footed boobies nest on the ground on islands in the South Pacific. They feed on fish and are good divers.

Blue-footed booby

Some plants, such as burdock, have seeds covered in many tiny hooks. They catch on bird feathers or animal fur and drop off much later.

Other plants, such as figs, produce fruit with seeds inside. Animals eat the fruit. The seeds later pass out in the animal droppings.

For an animal species to survive on a new island, the first animal to arrive must be able to breed* (produce young), so it needs to survive until a mate arrives.

Animals that can fly, such as birds, bats and insects, can cross water. They can easily land on new islands and start breeding.

Plant-eating animals can survive if they land on islands where there are plants to eat. They are the next animals to arrive on new islands, after the seals and sea-birds.

Land animals, such as squirrels, iguanas and toads, only cross the oceans if they are swept out to sea. This is rare, so they don't arrive very often on new islands. People think a new type of animal only came to Hawaii (an island in the Pacific) once every 12,500 years.

*Breeding, 16.

Island life

Over millions of years, animals and plants on many of the world's islands have developed differently from mainland ones. The older an island is, the more different its plants and animals are. Species that do not live elsewhere in the world are called endemic species.

Ancient plants and animals

Sometimes when a species of animal or plant has died out everywhere else, it may still be living on islands.

The only remaining tuataras live and breed in New Zealand. Fossils* of them have been found around the world. They are the same age as dinosaur fossils.

Tuatara

Tree ferns still grow on New Zealand's South Island today.

Coal contains fossils of plants, such as tree ferns, that grew everywhere in huge, swampy forests millions of years ago.

Successful animals

If animals arrive on islands with lots of food and few hunting animals, they survive to have young themselves. This has happened in the past and over thousands of years of breeding, many island animals have become different from their mainland relatives.

This tiny Seychelles gecko is much smaller than other geckos.

The fossa is a cat-like hunter, about the same size as a fox. It hunts small animals and birds. It is only found on one island off the coast of Africa, called Madagascar.

Fossa

On some islands, a few sea animals have become good at living on land. They first came to the land because there was plenty of food to eat.

The robber crab's ancestors were sea-living hermit crabs. It eats the insides of coconuts and can climb palm trees.

Giant lizards, called komodo dragons, live on two islands in Indonesia. They are the largest lizards in the world.

Komodo dragon

Robber crabs have a very tough shell which stops them from drying out in the air.

36   *Fossils, 4,

The arrival of people

In the past, people who settled on islands made many animals and plants die out.

They killed them for food, destroyed their homes or brought mainland species with them, which ate the island animals' food.

The New Zealand moa was a giant, flightless bird. It was nearly as tall as a giraffe and fed on leaves at the top of trees. It was hunted to extinction*.

Thylacines used to live in Tasmania. They were fiercely hunted by farmers because they killed the farmers' animals. They may have died out.

Millions of years ago lemurs lived in forests around the world. Today nearly all of them live on Madagascar, an island off Africa.

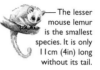

The lesser mouse lemur is the smallest species. It is only 11cm (4in) long without its tail.

The indri lemur is the largest kind. It grows to one meter (3ft) long.

Now the forests where the lemurs live are being cleared. Three quarters of the forests have disappeared in the last 50 years. Many species of lemur are now in danger of extinction.

On the Galapagos islands there are 14 species of finch. Each one has a beak specially shaped for the food it eats.

The large ground finch is a seed-eater with a short, thick beak for crushing tough seeds.

The vegetarian tree finch eats buds and fruit. It has a hooked beak, like a parrot. Parrots are also vegetarian.

The warbler finch looks very much like a warbler. It eats insects and has a small, pointed beak.

The woodpecker finch uses a cactus spine as a tool to dig out grubs from the bark.

The first pair of finches came to the islands to breed. Soon there were so many finches that they began to run out of food. Some of them had different shaped beaks. They survived because they could eat other foods. Over many years the 14 different species developed.

Flightless birds

Birds that cannot fly are quite common on islands. Scientists think they lose their ability to fly when there is plenty of food near the ground and also no need to escape because there are no predators (hunting animals). Several birds in New Zealand are flightless.

Kiwis eat worms, snails and other small, ground-living animals. They are the only birds with a good sense of smell (they use whiskers on their beaks).

The kakapo is a giant parrot. It feeds at night on leaves and berries close to the ground.

The takahe is a rare plant-eating bird that cannot fly. It is the size of a chicken and brilliantly colored.

Grasslands

Natural grasslands are flat, open and windy. The plants are mostly grasses and low bushes, but there are also sometimes a few trees. There are lots of plant-eaters, which in turn attract hunters.

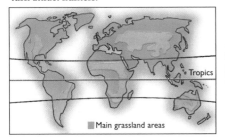

Tropics

Main grassland areas

Where are grasslands?

Grasslands cover a quarter of all the land on Earth. Grasses need less water to grow than trees, but most are killed by shade from taller plants. This is why most grasslands grow between forests and deserts.

Grasslands in the tropics have only two seasons, a rainy one and a dry one. It is hot all year round.

Temperate grasslands have the usual four seasons. It is warm in summer, but can be very cold in winter.

The African savannah

The largest remaining natural grasslands are in Africa. They have not been changed by people because of a tiny insect pest, the tse-tse fly, which spreads a disease called sleeping sickness. The disease has stopped people from clearing land and settling down as farmers. So the wild plants and animals are still there. Many of them are protected in huge areas, called **reserves**.

Tall grasses cover the land. After the rainy season, they dry out, catching fire easily. When the rain comes again, new leaves grow fast.

Tough, fire-resistant trees, such as acacia and baobab trees, grow in groups wherever there is enough water for them.

There are often lakes and marshy areas after the rainy season. These dry out fast, but larger numbers of trees and plants grow near them.

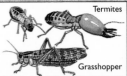

Meerkats stand up on their hind legs, resting on their tails, to see over the tall grass. One watches for danger while the others feed.

Millions of insects, such as grasshoppers, beetles, ants and termites, live among the tall grasses.

Termites

Grasshopper

Living together

On the flat, open grasslands, many animals live in groups for their protection. Different kinds of animal groups are organized in different ways.

Huge **herds** (groups) of wildebeest move over plains, feeding. Together they have more eyes, ears and noses to sense danger. The herd has no leader. New members join and others leave all the time.

Elephants live in herds that are more closely organized. The leader is usually an old female. The other females share tasks, such as caring for the calves. Males leave the group at 12 years old, but the females stay.

Baboons live in family groups called **troops**, which are very closely organized. Each troop is led by an older male. He keeps everyone together and defends them, with the help of younger males, if they are attacked.

Huge herds of large plant-eating animals, such as zebras, wander over the plains, eating the grass.

Vultures, marabou storks and other animals eat the hunter's scraps.

Many animals, such as servals, have long legs. This helps them see over the long grass.

Large hunting animals, such as lions, eat many plant-eating animals.

Grassland plants

The plants which grow in the grasslands are mainly different kinds of grasses. There are about 8,000 different species. All grassland plants have to be able to survive dry periods and having their leaves and shoots eaten. Most trees cannot do this very well.

Land plants and water

Most land plants take up water from the soil through their roots. They need water to make food in their leaves by photosynthesis*.

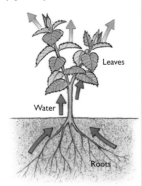

Leaves

Water

Roots

Inside the leaves some of the water turns into a gas called water vapor, which is lost into the air. Water always flows from the soil, through plants and into the air in this way.

If plants run out of water, they wilt at first, then they begin to dry out. If they get no more water, they die.

Coping with dry periods

Most trees are big plants. The bigger plants grow, the more water they need. Even with their long, deep roots, most trees would not be able to find enough water in grassland areas to survive.

Grasses are much smaller than trees and they also grow many long roots. These help them to find the little water there is on the grasslands. They can survive on this water because they need less than trees.

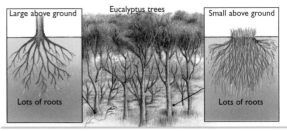

Large above ground

Eucalyptus trees

Small above ground

Lots of roots

Lots of roots

Coping with plant-eaters

Grasses grow long, straight leaves from near the ground which keep getting longer as the plant gets older. When the tips of the leaves are eaten by animals, the leaves continue growing from the bottom. This means that hungry, plant-eating animals are not a real danger to grasses.

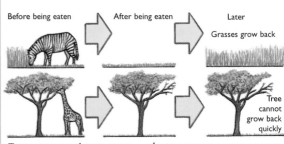

Before being eaten

After being eaten

Later

Grasses grow back

Tree cannot grow back quickly

Trees grow new leaves every year. At first their leaves grow quickly, then they stop growing. If they are eaten, the tree cannot grow new ones until next year. The trees need to stop animals from eating their new leaves.

There are some trees which can survive in areas such as grasslands, where there is little water.

Trees such as acacias, baobabs and eucalyptuses in Africa and Australia grow on grasslands. They have tough leaves that hold in water, like those on desert plants.

Pampas grass

Acacia trees

Baobab tree

Trees with tough leaves lose less water and so need less from the ground.

In very dry areas, only short grasses grow. In slightly wetter places, taller grasses can grow.

Many grassland trees store water in their trunks. Baobab trees store huge amounts and their trunks swell up. Many animals get water from them, for example, some elephants smash them open.

Thorn bush

Some plants, such as thorn bushes, grow sharp spines on their branches. Most animals avoid these prickly plant dinners.

Acacia tree

As well as having thorns, some acacia trees have leaves that make a nasty-tasting chemical when they are eaten. They soon taste so bad that plant-eaters, such as giraffes, go off to find a tastier meal.

Using grasses

Many food plants, such as wheat, oats, barley and rice are species of grass. Their ancestors were different, wild grass species.

Very early farmers chose seeds from wild plants with the biggest seeds.

They kept these seeds to plant the next year. Over many hundreds of years, modern food plants developed from early wild ones. These crops have many large seeds.

Modern oats

Modern wheat

Wild grass

Modern rye

The early farmers chose plants whose seeds stayed on the plant. Modern crops are easy to harvest because the seeds do not drop.

Grassland plant-eaters

Large grassland areas provide enough food for lots of herbivores (plant-eating animals). These animals can live together because they all eat slightly different things.

Browsers and grazers

Animals such as giraffes, elephants, black rhinos and some antelopes eat leaves from trees and bushes. They are called **browsers**. Other animals, such as wildebeest, zebras and hippos, eat grass. They are called **grazers**.

The giraffe's long neck helps it reach the leaves at the very top of trees.

Elephants can reach leaves nearly as high as giraffes. They also eat young grass shoots in the rainy season.

Kudus feed on leaves which grow at the same height as their heads.

Black rhinos have a pointed top lip, to help them pull leaves from bushes at head height.

Gerenuks can stand on their hind legs to reach leaves. No other hooved animals can do this.

Small antelopes such as the dik dik eat leaves which grow close to the ground.

Migrations

The best food for grazing animals is the new grass which grows in spring or the rainy season. As the seasons change, many grassland animals make long journeys, called **migrations**, to find this food.

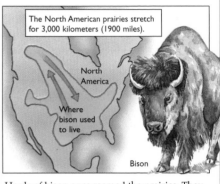

The North American prairies stretch for 3,000 kilometers (1900 miles).

North America

Where bison used to live

Bison

Herds of bison once roamed the prairies. They spent winter in the south, where it was warmer and easier to find food. Then they followed the spring north, returning south again in autumn.

42

Plants as food

To get energy from their food, animals need to **digest** it (break it up into simple substances inside their bodies). On grasslands, most plant-eaters feed on grass and leaves which are tough and difficult to digest. To survive, they need to eat lots and be good at digesting their food.

Plant-eaters need to chew their food a lot to get it ready to be digested.

Jaw moves sideways

They have grinding teeth and jaws that move from side to side.

Teeth grind food

Some plant-eaters, such as giraffes and bison, have a stomach in two main parts, instead of just one. Their food goes to each part in turn. This means they can digest tough, partly digested food a second time, to get the energy from it.

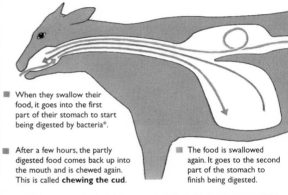

■ When they swallow their food, it goes into the first part of their stomach to start being digested by bacteria*.

■ After a few hours, the partly digested food comes back up into the mouth and is chewed again. This is called **chewing the cud**.

■ The food is swallowed again. It goes to the second part of the stomach to finish being digested.

Zebras like to eat fairly short grasses, but they will eat new grass of most kinds.

Wildebeest prefer short grasses. Zebras and wildebeest often graze together.

White rhinos eat the shoots at ground level. They have a flat top lip.

At night, hippos graze on grass on land. As well as normal teeth for munching grass, they have an extra pair of huge, front teeth. They use them to defend their homes and fight for females.

*Bacteria, 113.

Grassland meat-eaters

Large numbers of herbivores (plant-eaters) on grasslands mean lots of food for carnivores (meat-eaters). Meat is a rich food and much easier to digest* than plants. Carnivores do not need to eat as often as plant-eaters. They spend a lot more time resting or sleeping.

Types of carnivores

Predators are hunting animals. They only eat fresh meat: the animals that they have killed. These animals are their **prey**.

Animals that eat meat they have not killed are **scavengers.** They pick clean the bodies of animals that died naturally and the remains of predators' kills.

Hunting dog   Eagle   Lion

All predators have good eyesight. Their eyes are close together in the front of their heads. This helps them judge how far away their prey is, so they can catch it more easily.

Some eagles can spot prey from over eight kilometers (five miles) away.

African savannah predators

African hunting dogs live in groups, called **packs**. The adults hunt together, wearing out large prey, such as wildebeest, by chasing them over very long distances. They share the food.

Leopard

Lions are the only cats that live in family groups. These groups are called **prides**. The females hunt together, often **stalking** (creeping up on) their prey for several hours.

A pride of lions

Cheetahs hunt alone. They sprint after their prey at up to 100kph (60mph), but they soon get tired. Unless they kill within a minute, they give up.

Leopards hunt alone and at night. They kill more than they can eat in one meal, and store their kills in trees, to come back to later.

Cheetah sprinting

*Digest, 43.

Snakes

Snakes eat small animals, birds and eggs. Many are too slow to chase their prey, so instead they hide and wait for a meal to pass. Different kinds of snakes kill their prey in different ways.

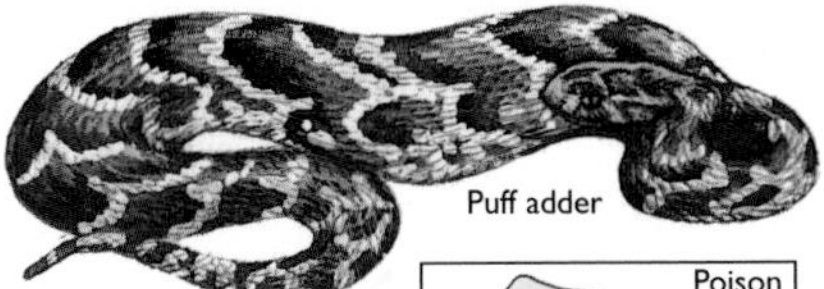

Puff adder

Snakes such as pythons suffocate their prey. They are called **constrictors**. They wrap themselves around their prey and squeeze hard. The prey soon runs out of breath and dies.

Snakes such as puff adders poison their prey. They bite them with teeth, called **fangs**, that drip poison, called **venom**.

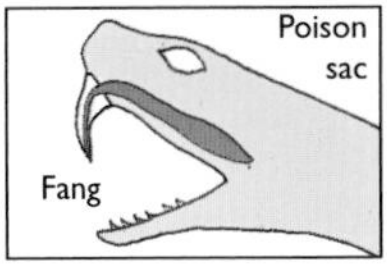

Poison sac

Fang

Python

Snakes open their jaws very wide and swallow their prey whole. Then they find a quiet place to digest the meal and only hunt again when they are hungry. A big meal might last a python for several weeks.

Scavengers

Some animals, such as vultures, are always scavengers. Others hunt most of the time but will scavenge when there is less food around.

Vulture

White-backed vulture

White-backed vultures have a weak beak. They cannot feed until another animal has ripped the skin.

Hyena

White-headed vultures can rip open skin to get at the meat inside.

Secretary bird

White-headed vulture

Hyenas have very strong necks and mouths, used for crushing bones. They kill small antelopes but scavenge as well when food is scarce.

Secretary birds hunt and scavenge. They kill and eat small animals, such as snakes.

Survival on the grasslands

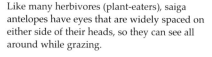

There are few hiding places for all the large plant-eating animals on the flat, open grasslands. Some can hide by crouching in the grass or bushes, or burrowing underground, but most are too big. All grassland animals have ways of looking out for predators (hunters). Different animals have different ways of avoiding being caught and eaten.

Looking out for predators

Many grassland animals, such as antelopes, gather in herds for their protection. Together they have more eyes, ears and noses to sense a hunting animal's approach.

Saiga antelopes live on the steppes in central Asia.

Like many herbivores (plant-eaters), saiga antelopes have eyes that are widely spaced on either side of their heads, so they can see all around while grazing.

Saiga　　　　Rabbit　　　　Rhea

Getting away

Many animals in different places run away from hunters, but on grasslands it is especially important because there are few hiding places.

Animals such as antelopes need to run faster than their hunters to survive. Hunters such as coyotes need to be fast in order to catch their food.

Pronghorn antelope

Coyote

Knee
Ankle
Toe
Knee

All fast runners run on their toes. Their ankle is half-way up their leg and their knee is close to their body.

Hoofs or claws stick into the ground and stop animals from slipping, in the same way that spikes on running shoes help an athlete to run more quickly.

Jumpers

Kangaroos jump instead of run.

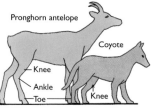

Kangaroos have huge back legs.

They balance with their stiff tails.

The red kangaroo can jump 14m (42ft).

Size and armor

If an animal is big enough or well protected enough, hunters will usually try not to kill it. For example, rhinos and elephants are so big that no other animals hunt them. Only people hunt them for their tusks and horns.

Rhino

Rhinos have thick skin for extra protection. They are short-sighted, but have a good sense of smell. If they feel threatened by anything, they charge.

Giraffe

Young giraffes are big, but they are sometimes attacked. An adult, though, can kill a lion with one kick.

Lion

Armadillo

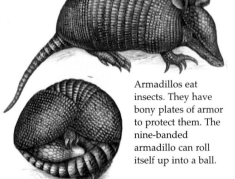

Armadillos eat insects. They have bony plates of armor to protect them. The nine-banded armadillo can roll itself up into a ball.

Blending in with the background

Some animals blend in with their background and so are harder for predators to spot. This is a common way of hiding, known as **camouflage**.

Many grassland antelopes, such as Thompson's gazelles, have sandy colored backs. This helps them to blend in with their background, making it hard for hunters to spot them.

Many birds, such as the female sage grouse, are dull coloured. A female on her nest on the ground is hard to see and only flies off if hunters come too close. In spring, the males have brightly colored feathers to attract females, but they shed them later.

Ostriches, rheas and emus are all large flightless birds. They can run very fast to escape the few predators that are large enough to attack them. They are all dull colored as well, except the black and white male ostrich, which is the largest bird in the world.

Rhea   Emu   Ostrich

47

Life underground

There is little shelter on grasslands and many different kinds of small animals have solved this by living underground. Some feed on plants or smaller animals above ground and only use their homes for shelter. Others spend all their lives underground.

Burrowing for shelter

Many animals that live underground only use their burrows for shelter. They live in groups and come up to the surface to feed.

Grasslands are home to large numbers of burrowing **rodents**. These are mammals*, such as rats, squirrels and beavers, which have gnawing teeth. They have many young, several times a year and are food for many animals.

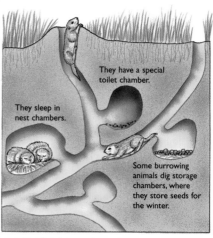

Black-bellied hamsters live on the steppes. They feed on seeds and leaves.

Prairie dogs live in North America. They eat seeds, grasses and roots.

Maras (also called Patagonian hares) are South American. They eat grass.

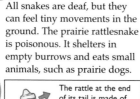

Prairie rattlesnake

All snakes are deaf, but they can feel tiny movements in the ground. The prairie rattlesnake is poisonous. It shelters in empty burrows and eats small animals, such as prairie dogs.

The rattle at the end of its tail is made of pieces of dead skin. When threatened, it shakes them to make a loud warning sound.

Living in groups

Many burrowing animals, such as prairie dogs, dig burrows with many connecting tunnels, several exits and many different chambers. They live together in groups and share the work.

They have a special toilet chamber.

They sleep in nest chambers.

Some burrowing animals dig storage chambers, where they store seeds for the winter.

Burrowing owls

Meerkats

American burrowing owls often nest in old burrows. Their chicks' call sounds like the rattle of a prairie rattlesnake. This may deter other hunters.

Meerkats live in family groups. The older ones help to take care of the young ones and take turns to keep a look out, while the others hunt for food or doze.

Insect colonies

Insects such as ants and termites live in huge groups called **colonies**. All the members of the colony hatch from eggs laid by one female, the **queen**. Termite nests have thick walls and the air is warm and damp inside, like a burrow.

Some termites, called **workers**, build the nest and collect rotting plants to feed the colony.

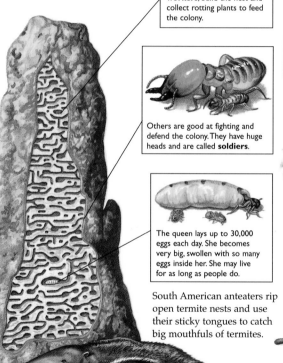

Others are good at fighting and defend the colony. They have huge heads and are called **soldiers**.

The queen lays up to 30,000 eggs each day. She becomes very big, swollen with so many eggs inside her. She may live for as long as people do.

South American anteaters rip open termite nests and use their sticky tongues to catch big mouthfuls of termites.

Naked mole rats

Naked mole rats are one of the few mamma species that live in colonies with a queen, workers and soldiers, just as insects do.

They are African rodents that spend all their lives under the ground. They are almost blind and feed on plant roots.

Aardwolf

Aardwolves are African. They have very weak teeth and feed on insects. They often shelter in old burrows.

Baby aardvark

The aardvark is African. It is the largest burrowing animal in the world. It can grow up to two meters (6ft) long and uses its sticky tongue to catch termites. It is very shy and only comes out at night.

49

Deserts

One-seventh of all the land on Earth is desert. Deserts are very dry areas which get less than 25cm (10in) of rain each year. Most deserts, such as the Sahara in Africa, are hot, but there are cold deserts near the poles (see page 72), where the water is frozen for most of the year.

Day and night

Most hot deserts heat up fast during the day and cool down quickly at night. At midday it can be very hot, but by midnight the temperature may be nearly freezing.

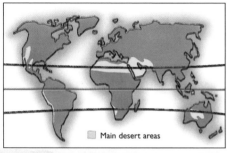

Main desert areas

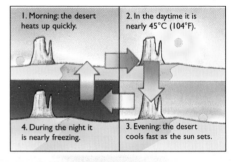

1. Morning: the desert heats up quickly.

2. In the daytime it is nearly 45°C (104°F).

4. During the night it is nearly freezing.

3. Evening: the desert cools fast as the sun sets.

Life in a hot desert

It is difficult to tell where grasslands finish and deserts begin, because there are areas at the edge of deserts where grasses and bushes grow. In other areas, though, there are large patches of dry earth, rock or sand between plants and in some places no plants can grow at all. Some types of desert animals can survive in even the harshest conditions.

Strong, dry winds wear away rocks into strange shapes and blow sand and soil around. In some places, there are large areas of bare rock.

Red-tailed hawk

Hunting birds, such as owls and falcons, can live in deserts. Desert birds' feathers keep them cool in the daytime and warm at night (see page 55).

In some places sand piles up, making sand dunes. Few plants can grow on dunes because the sand is nearly always moving.

At the edges of deserts a few grasses, bushes and desert plants, such as cacti, grow.

Water in deserts

The little rain that does fall in deserts often comes in short, violent storms. The rainwater soaks into the ground quickly, dries up, or is carried away along old river beds.

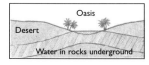

Sand dunes

Oases

Sand grouse

There is water underground almost everywhere, trapped in certain kinds of rock (see page 84). In deserts this water is usually deep underground, but in a few places, called **oases**, the rocks are at the surface.

Plants such as date palms, that cannot grow elsewhere in deserts, can grow near oases, as their roots can reach the water.

Many desert birds, such as sand grouse, and larger desert animals, such as foxes, visit oases regularly to drink.

Lizards are very good at surviving the heat and dryness in deserts. Many feed on insects.

A few large hunters, such as foxes and cats, can survive in deserts. They feed on many different small animals.

Kit fox

Many insects, such as ants, beetles, moths and locusts live in deserts. They are food for many animals.

Many desert animals, such as kangaroo rats, avoid the hottest part of the day by getting out of the sun. They burrow underground and feed at night when it's cooler.

51

Coping with the dryness

All animals and plants need water to survive and grow, but rain does not always fall every year in deserts.

In the driest parts, no plants grow and few animals can survive. But in other areas some plants and animals have special ways of coping with the long dry periods.

In the Central Australian Desert rain only falls about once every five or six years.

Plants and water

Some desert plants have long roots to find water hidden deep underground. Others make the most of the short rainy periods, storing water inside parts of themselves when there is lots of water around.

Mesquite bushes have roots that grow up to 30m (100ft) long to reach deep underground water.

Most plants in other places lose lots of water through their leaves, but desert plants must save water. Some of them have special "watertight" leaves. Other plants lose their leaves in dry periods.

Welwitschia from Africa store their water in a huge root underground. Their long leaves have a special thick "skin" which stops water from getting out.

Water for the animals

All animals get some water from their food and this is enough for many small desert animals. But most birds and larger animals, such as camels and foxes, also need to visit waterholes to drink. Some of them can last a long time between drinks and they save as much water as possible.

Budgerigars

Many desert birds, such as Australian budgerigars, gather to drink at waterholes in huge flocks every morning.

Most animals lose lots of water in their droppings. Camels have very dry droppings. This helps them save water and last for days between drinks.

When they reach water, camels can drink 123 liters (27 gallons) in ten minutes. This is about two-thirds of a bathtub full.

Camel

Saguaro cacti have a spongy stem which swells up full of water after a rainy period. Most plants make food in their leaves. Cacti do not have leaves. They can make food in their green stems instead.

Cactus spines are dead and hard to stop water from being lost. They also protect the plant from being eaten by animals.

Sometimes dew (drops of water from the air) forms on the cacti. The water runs down to the ground and is taken up by the roots.

The ocotillo cannot store water, but it can make food in its green stem, as well as in its leaves. As soon as the rainwater begins to dry up it drops its leaves to save water.

Ocotillo after rain falls

Ocotillo once rain dries up

Many desert rodents*, such as gerbils, never need to drink. They get water from their food and lose only a little water in their very dry droppings.

Gerbil

Hunting animals and birds, such as coyotes, roadrunners and shrikes, get some water from the bodies of their prey, but they still have to drink.

Shrike

Shrike spear their prey on to thorny branches, so that it is easier to eat.

All reptiles* and insects have a thick skin that stops water from being lost from inside their bodies. This means they need less water. Many of them do not need to drink.

The Australian stumpy-tailed or shingle-back lizard stores fat in its tail, as a source of energy and water.

Namib beetle

The African Namib beetle lives in a desert where it almost never rains. Fog drifts in over the desert and the water in the fog turns into dew on the beetle's body. It drinks this by tilting itself, so that the drops run down its body into its mouth.

*Reptiles, 116; Rodents, 48.

Coping with desert temperatures

Desert animals have to be able to cope with the huge changes in temperature each day. Different kinds of animals do this in different ways. Lots of them take shelter during the worst times of day. Some others have special things about their bodies to help them survive.

Body temperature

All animals move around and hunt for food best when their bodies are at a certain temperature. This "best" temperature is different for different kinds of animals.

Desert
Roadrunner

Antarctic

Some animals, such as insects and reptiles*, are called **cold-blooded** animals. Their bodies are always warmer than their surroundings. If it is cold, they are cold. If it is warm, they are warm. When they begin to get too cold they move to a warmer place. When they get too hot, they move to a cooler place. They have to do this because if their bodies get too cold or too hot, they will die.

Cold-blooded animals, such as lizards, sunbathe in the morning to warm up.

Lizards move into the shade when it gets too hot.

Other animals, such as birds and mammals*, can keep themselves at their "best" temperature all the time. They are called **warm-blooded**

Marsupial mice

animals. They use the energy they get from food to make heat to warm their bodies. They cool down by losing water from their skin, or **sweating**.

Warm-blooded desert animals, such as Australian marsupial* mice, can hunt for food at night even though it is very cold. They can do this because of the heat they make inside themselves.

Keeping cool

Warm-blooded animals can control their body temperature, but they cannot afford to lose too much water keeping cool. In the desert in the hottest part of the day, many of them move into the shade, like cold-blooded animals do.

Fennec fox

The African fennec fox spends the day resting in burrows. It comes out to hunt for food at night. It can hear very well with its huge ears and this helps it hunt in the darkness.

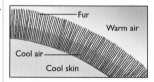
Fur
Warm air
Cool air
Cool skin

As with all furry animals, its fur keeps it warm in the cold, but also helps it keep cool in the heat. The fur traps a layer of air which stops cold air from reaching its warm skin, or hot air from reaching its cool skin.

*Mammals, Marsupials, Reptiles, 116.

Some peccaries live in American deserts. They spend the hottest part of the day resting in the shade in order to save water. They also scrape shallow holes in the soil to lie in.

Peccaries

Like fennec foxes, American jackrabbits have large ears with lots of blood vessels close to the surface. Animals lose heat into the air from surface blood vessels, so the more there are the more heat can be lost.

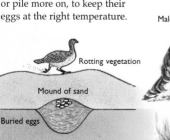

Jackrabbit

Blood vessels

Birds have to protect their eggs from getting too hot. Malee fowl bury their eggs in rotting vegetation under mounds of sand and keep testing how hot it is inside. They scrape away sand or pile more on, to keep their eggs at the right temperature.

Birds' feathers help them to keep cool in the heat as well as warm in the cold, in the same way that fur does for animals.

Rotting vegetation

Mound of sand

Buried eggs

Malee fowl

Large animals

The few large, warm-blooded animals cannot burrow under the ground to get out of the heat and there isn't enough shade to keep them cool.

Instead they can let their bodies heat up past their "best" temperature during the day and cool down past it at night. Other smaller animals would suffer if they did this.

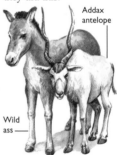

Addax antelope

Wild ass

They have pale colored coats because pale colors do not heat up as quickly in bright sunshine as dark ones.

Camel

Camels are often bad-tempered. This may happen when they get too hot.

Rain in the desert

After rain falls in the desert, many plants flower and new plants grow quickly from seeds under the ground. Animals that have hidden underground during the long dry periods come out to feed on the new plants, and to produce their young.

Insects feed on plants and at the same time pollinate* the new flowers, which then make thousands of new seeds. Many of these seeds and new young animals are eaten by other animals, but a few survive.

Desert toads and shrimps

Toads need water to lay their eggs in and shrimps live in water. Millions of years ago, some deserts were covered in water and many toads and shrimps lived there. Over thousands of years, the water dried up, but a few kinds of toads and shrimps changed so that they could cope with the dryness. There are still desert toads and shrimps today.

The spadefoot toad digs itself underground to survive the dryness. It comes out when it rains, to mate and lay its eggs.

Insect life

All insects lay eggs. In some cases, such as flies and moths, the young that hatch look very different from the adults. For more about these, see pages 62-63. The young of other insects, such as locusts, look similar to the adults, but do not have wings. Many desert animals eat them.

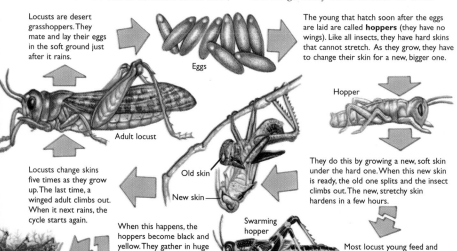

Locusts are desert grasshoppers. They mate and lay their eggs in the soft ground just after it rains.

Eggs

The young that hatch soon after the eggs are laid are called **hoppers** (they have no wings). Like all insects, they have hard skins that cannot stretch. As they grow, they have to change their skin for a new, bigger one.

Hopper

Adult locust

Old skin

New skin

Locusts change skins five times as they grow up. The last time, a winged adult climbs out. When it next rains, the cycle starts again.

They do this by growing a new, soft skin under the hard one. When this new skin is ready, the old one splits and the insect climbs out. The new, stretchy skin hardens in a few hours.

When this happens, the hoppers become black and yellow. They gather in huge groups, called **swarms**. Then they march in search of food. They eat any plants they find and do great damage to crops.

Swarming hopper

Most locust young feed and live by themselves. Sometimes, though, many hoppers find themselves close to each other and short of food.

*Pollination, 14.

Flowers in the desert

Many desert plants produce their flowers after rain. Some plants first grow quickly, from tough seeds that have lain in the ground during the long, dry period. The flowers produce lots of new seeds before the rain-water dries up.

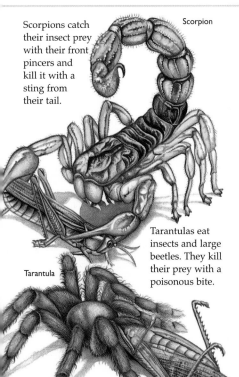

Desert shrimp eggs survive in dried-up mud until it rains. Then the shrimps hatch, grow up fast and lay their eggs in puddles before they die.

The Australian sungold grows quickly, covering the ground after rain falls.

North American century plants grow for about 15 years before flowering. Then when it rains, they flower and produce seeds very fast. New plants grow from the seeds. The old plants die.

Scorpions catch their insect prey with their front pincers and kill it with a sting from their tail.

Scorpion

Tarantulas eat insects and large beetles. They kill their prey with a poisonous bite.

Tarantula

Growing deserts

Plants are very important in dry areas. Their roots soak up any rain that falls and trap the soil, stopping it from being blown or washed away.

In the 1920s, large areas of American grassland were cleared for farmland.

Later there were several hot, dry years in a row. The crops died. Farmers kept on plowing their fields to plant new crops and the soil became very dry.

Strong winds blew away so much of the soil that no new plants could grow, even in the wet years. The area became a "desert", called the Dust Bowl.

In the last 100 years the area of "desert" around the world has doubled. Some places have become desert because the weather has changed. Others, such as the Dust Bowl in America, have changed because the plants were cleared and the soil destroyed. If too many people try to farm or graze their animals in very dry areas then even more land may become desert.

Temperate forests

Nearly a third of the land surface on Earth is covered by forests. Forests grow naturally wherever there is enough water for trees to grow and are home to many other plants and lots of animals. Temperate forests are ones that grow between the tropics and polar regions.

Types of trees

There are two main kinds of trees, deciduous and evergreen trees.

Deciduous trees shed all their leaves at one time, so they are bare for part of the year. They rest during this time. They grow new leaves when there is enough sun and rain for them to grow.

Deciduous trees shed their leaves and rest for part of the year.

Evergreen trees keep their leaves for several years and lose them gradually, while growing new ones, so they are never bare.

Which trees grow where?

The biggest, most common species of trees in a forest is called the **dominant species**. Different species can survive different amounts of cold and dryness, so temperate forests have different dominant species in different areas.

Evergreen forest

Deciduous forest

Mountain forests (see page 79)

In Polar regions, no trees grow because it is too cold and all the water is frozen as ice.

Just south of the Arctic Circle there are huge evergreen forests. The dominant species, such as pine, fir and spruce, can survive freezing winters.

Tropic of Cancer

Seasons

All temperate areas have four seasons. The trees and most other forest plants grow in a yearly cycle. They grow new leaves in spring, flowers and new leaf-buds in summer and seeds in the autumn. The lives of forest animals follow a yearly cycle too.

In spring the trees grow new leaves. Many animals produce their young.

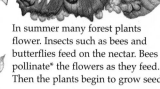

In summer many forest plants flower. Insects such as bees and butterflies feed on the nectar. Bees pollinate* the flowers as they feed. Then the plants begin to grow seeds.

*Pollination, 14.

Deciduous trees, such as beech, oak and maple, grow best where summers are warm and winters not too cold. They grow in a broad band across Asia, Europe and North America.

Caring for forests

Two thousand years ago, forests covered a lot of Europe, America and Asia, but most have now been lost. For instance, less than 10% of Britain's forests are left.

As the number of people grew, more and more wanted to live on the land and farm crops, so they cut down the forests.

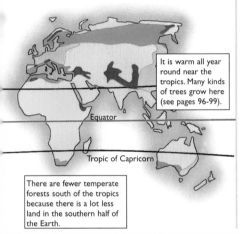

Equator

It is warm all year round near the tropics. Many kinds of trees grow here (see pages 96-99).

Tropic of Capricorn

There are fewer temperate forests south of the tropics because there is a lot less land in the southern half of the Earth.

They still needed wood for building and other uses. They found if they chopped down trees, such as hazel, but left stumps with roots in the ground, the trees grew new stems quickly.

They cut off these stems every few years, though some trees were left to grow naturally. There were trees of many different ages and many animals lived among them.

Today, many people farm fast-growing evergreen trees instead. They plant hundreds of new young trees in huge areas. These are not true forests, because all the trees are the same kind. Few animals can live in them.

In autumn, many animals, such as European badgers, feast on ripe fruit, berries and seeds. They store up food, which they can use during winter. Deciduous trees shed their leaves.

In winter, deciduous trees are bare and there is little food for animals. Many of them migrate (make long journeys) to warmer winter feeding grounds. Others hibernate (rest) until spring.

Deciduous forests

Most temperate deciduous forests grow in Europe, Asia or North America where summers are long and warm, and winters are not too cold. They are home to huge numbers of animals, many of which are tiny insects. One oak tree can house over 4,000 species, including plants, insects and other animals.

Deciduous trees

There are many different kinds of deciduous trees. Most have broad, flat leaves and their seeds grow inside a case. Berries and fruits that people eat, such as plums, apples, figs and oranges, are all cases with seeds inside. Many seeds grow inside other kinds of cases, too.

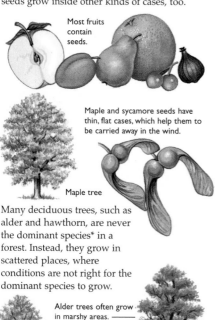

Most fruits contain seeds.

Maple and sycamore seeds have thin, flat cases, which help them to be carried away in the wind.

Maple tree

Many deciduous trees, such as alder and hawthorn, are never the dominant species* in a forest. Instead, they grow in scattered places, where conditions are not right for the dominant species to grow.

Alder trees often grow in marshy areas.

Birch trees are very tough. They can grow a long way farther north than most other deciduous trees.

A European oak forest

Oak trees are the dominant species* in oak forests. Their flat, broad, delicate leaves let some light filter through to the forest floor, where many smaller plants grow.

The forest is made up of different layers of plants. Many animals find their food in only one or two layers of the forest; others can move between all the layers.

The roof of the forest is made up of the leaves and branches of the tallest trees. This part of the forest is called the **canopy**.

Small trees and bushes grow between the oaks. This is called the **shrub layer**. Some of them, such as holly and rhododendron, are evergreen.

Small mammals* and birds, such as woodmice, wrens and nightingales, live in the shrub layer. Many male birds sing in spring to attract females.

Woodmouse

Wren

The trees lose their leaves in autumn. Huge amounts of leaf litter (dead plant material) build up on the ground under the trees.

*Dominant species, 58; Mammals, 116.

Many insects live in the canopy, feeding on wood, leaves, flowers and seeds.

Weevil   Butterfly

Many birds, such as jays, build their nests in the canopy and feed on plant material or insects.

Old dead trees are often used for shelter by birds, such as owls and other forest animals.

Owl

There are trees of all different ages in a forest. When an old tree dies and falls down, more light gets through into the clearing that is made. Many bushes and new young trees grow quickly to fill the gap.

A few plants, such as ferns, mosses, algae and lichens, grow on the trunks of the oak trees.

Squirrels move between the layers by running up and down tree trunks.

Only adult male deer have antlers. They grow a new pair each summer.

Many young forest animals, such as deer, have spotted coats that blend into the background of light and shade in a forest. This helps them to hide from hunters.

Small streams run through the forest. Different plants, such as willow trees and rushes grow on the banks where the ground is much wetter.

61

Up in the canopy

In the spring and summer, the leafy canopy of a deciduous forest traps sunshine to make food for the trees. The trees use this food to grow. The canopy fills up with insects. Many of them feed on the new plant material. They are hunted by larger animals and birds.

Thousands of insects

Every deciduous tree is home to many different kinds of insects. Many adult insects lay their eggs in spring or early summer. They lay them on or close to the kind of food that their young eat. This means when their young hatch there is lots of food for them.

Ichneuman wasp young are carnivores (they eat meat). The adults lay their eggs in wood-tunnelling grubs. They use a long pointed tube to inject their eggs through the wood.

Ichneuman wasp

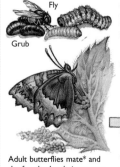

Pointed tube

Grub

When the wasp young hatch they eat the grub's insides. They come out through the grub's skin when they are fully grown. The grub dies.

No one really knows how the adult insects manage to find the wood-tunnelling grubs under the bark.

Pointed tube

Insect life

Some insect young, such as those of locusts and aphids, look similar to their parents. Others, such as grubs and caterpillars, look very different. They are called larvae*.

Fly

Grub

Caterpillars are the larvae of butterflies and moths. Grubs are the larvae of flies and beetles.

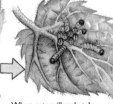

Adult butterflies mate* and the females lay their eggs on or close to the kind of food that their young eat.

When caterpillars hatch, they are tiny. They have strong jaws and start eating leaves right away.

Aphids and shield bugs have a hollow tube instead of a mouth. They suck up plant juices, called **sap**.

Aphid

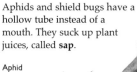

Shield bugs

Rolled-up beech leaf

The beech roller moth lays its eggs in a rolled-up beech leaf.

As they eat, they grow. Their skins cannot stretch, so they keep growing new larger ones under the old one, which then splits and falls off.

The last time a caterpillar sheds its skin, the new skin quickly hardens. It is now a pupa. Inside it changes into an adult.

When the hard skin of the pupa splits, the adult butterfly comes out. It rests for a short time, while its soft wings swell up and harden, before flying off.

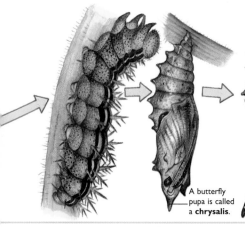

The whole process of change is called **metamorphosis**.

A butterfly pupa is called a **chrysalis**.

In temperate forests, many insects spend winter as a pupa. The adults come out in spring. But insects vary a lot. Some adults live for several years, so there may be larvae, pupae and adults in the canopy at the same time.

Some tiny insects, called leaf miners, lay their eggs into the middle of a leaf.

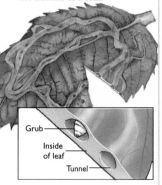

Grub

Inside of leaf

Tunnel

Their tiny young tunnel their way through the inside of the leaf, by eating it. The tunnels show up as winding line patterns on the leaf.

Birds and other animals

Many birds and animals live and feed in the canopy. They have home patches, or **territories**, which they defend from rivals that might compete for food, places to live or mates.

For most of the year, groups of long-tailed tits fly around in a forest looking for food. They keep together by calling to each other.

Long-tailed tits

Woodpecker

Flying squirrel

Woodpeckers nest in tree holes and feed on insects under bark or in soil. Their toes point in front and behind to help them to walk up tree trunks.

Flying squirrels from Europe, Asia and North America have flaps of skin on either side of their body. These help them to glide from tree to tree.

The forest floor

In deciduous forests, large amounts of dead leaves and wood fall to the ground every autumn. This forms the leaf litter. By the beginning of spring it has nearly all rotted away and the trees are growing new leaves. Many smaller plants grow between the trees. They make up the undergrowth and provide food and shelter for small and large animals.

Leaf litter animals

Many tiny animals, such as millipedes, beetles, woodlice and slugs, live among the leaf litter. They feed on the dead and rotting leaves and wood.

Slugs and snails scrape at their food with their rough tongues. They usually come out to feed at night.

Many other insects, such as beetles, feed on dead wood.

Woodlouse

Millipede

Millipedes and woodlice feed on dead plants mainly. They spend the day under stones in damp earth.

Earthworms mix up the soil. They tunnel under the ground eating soil as they go.

Hunters on the forest floor

Hunters on the forest floor are all different sizes. Many of the tiny ones, such as spiders, are eaten by larger ones, such as shrews or foxes. Some forest hunters, such as bears, eat both meat and plants. They are **omnivores**.

Centipedes have a pair of poison claws. They use them to kill or stun their prey.

Centipede

Woodcocks eat worms. They rarely fly, but the pattern of their feathers helps them hide among the dead leaves on the ground.

Woodcock

Hedgehog

Moles can dig fast with their large front feet. They feed on worms and insect larvae* underground. They have very poor eyesight, but they can hear well.

Hedgehogs eat worms, snails and insects. When threatened, they roll their bodies up into a tight ball.

Mole

How things rot

Rotting is when dead plants and animals are turned back into very simple substances by **fungi** and tiny living things called bacteria*. The substances, such as nitrates*, are then used by plants to grow new parts. In this way, they are always being recycled (see pages 12-13).

Cap

Stalk

Bacteria are too small to see, but there are millions in a teaspoonful of soil.

For most of the year, fungi are just tiny white threads in the soil. In autumn, many fungi grow a tall part with a cap and a stalk.

Mushrooms and toadstools are the tall parts. They make masses of tiny particles called **spores**, which blow away and grow into new fungi.

For more about fungi, see page 117.

Young opossums cling to their mother's fur.

Skunks are related to weasels. They feed on insects, eggs, mice and dead animals remains. If threatened they squirt a nasty smelling liquid at attackers.

Some kinds of skunks do a handstand just before squirting liquid.

Racoon

Opossums feed on small forest floor animals, but they can also climb trees. Their tails, like some monkeys' tails, can grip things.

Wild boar use their tusks to scrape for roots, fungi and tiny animals in the leaf litter. Sometimes, they kill small animals with their tusks.

Young wild boar have striped coats.

Racoons eat berries and nuts from the forest floor. They also fish from forest rivers. They hide and sleep in trees. They are distant relatives of pandas.

*Bacteria, 113; Nitrates, 13.

65

Northern evergreen forests

North of the deciduous forests there are huge forests of evergreen trees, which cover nearly one tenth of the Earth's surface. The trees, such as pine, fir, hemlock and spruce are all types of conifers. In the northernmost parts of these conifer forests, where conditions are harshest, the trees are smallest. Beyond them is the tundra* where no trees can grow.

What are conifers?

Conifers do not produce flowers, but they still produce seeds. They are called conifers because they all grow their seeds inside cones, instead of inside fruit. There is a seed between each scale of the cone.

Norway spruce cone

Conifers have tough leaves, called needles, which can survive the icy winters.

Scale

Most northern conifer trees are also shaped like cones. This means that snow slips off them more easily so the branches do not break under its weight.

Inside a conifer forest

Conifer needles rot very slowly and the soil is much poorer than the soil in a deciduous forest. The needles also grow close together on the branches and little light filters through to the forest floor. These things mean that only a few plants can grow between the trees.

Squirrels eat plants, conifer seeds and even birds' eggs. Most of the birds feed on the insects.

Only a few different kinds of insects, such as pine saw flies, live in the canopy, but there are lots of them. Their young feed on the needles.

Large areas of northern Canada are covered in almost untouched conifer forest.

It is dark inside the forest. Only small plants such as fungi, mosses and lichens grow on the forest floor.

Spruce grouse eat conifer needles.

Acid rain

Huge areas of conifer forests in Europe and North America are sick and dying. Many people think that pollution from the air is harming the trees.

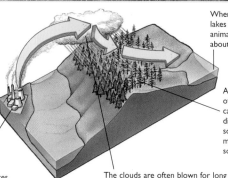

When acids are washed into lakes and rivers, they harm the animals living there (for more about how, see page 87).

Acid rain harms the surface of needles, so that the trees can be killed by pests and diseases more easily. It also soaks into the earth and makes the soil poisonous, so trees cannot grow.

Air pollution from car exhausts, factories and power stations contains chemicals such as sulfur. These turn into substances called **acids** inside clouds.

The clouds are often blown for long distances. The acids fall in rain or snow a long way away. This is called **acid rain** or **acid snow**.

Hunting birds and animals of all sizes, from shrews to lynx, live in the forest.

Great grey owl

Beavers chop down trees near rivers to make their homes (for more about them, see page 90). In the process, they flood areas within the forest. The soil is rich in these marshy areas and lots of grasses and flowers grow.

Many plant-eating animals, such as moose (called elk in Europe), hares, lemmings and voles, feed on the juicy plants in and around the lakes.

Winter in the northern forests

Seasons in the northern forests are very like those on the tundra*. Summers are cool, but the days are long, which means plants can grow fast. For most of the rest of the year it is icy and the days are short. Some animals live in the forests all year, but many others come and go.

Finding plants to eat

A few animals can get enough energy to survive by eating conifer needles, bark or seeds. This means they have a year-round food supply. Most animals, though, prefer the juicier plants in clearings and marshy areas. These grow quickly in summer but are covered in snow in winter.

Porcupine

Capercaillie

Capercaillies eat conifer needles. They have to spend nearly all day eating, to get enough from their poor food.

Porcupines eat tree bark. They prefer the soft young bark at the tips of branches and are good climbers.

Hunting animals

Because it is difficult to find food in winter, plant-eaters have to spread out and live alone, or in small groups. So hunters need large territories* to find enough food to survive.

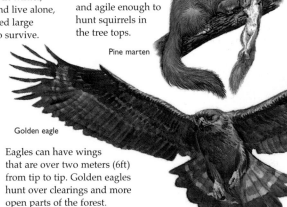

Pine martens are fast and agile enough to hunt squirrels in the tree tops.

Pine marten

Wolverines hunt birds and other small animals, but they are very fierce and will challenge a bear or a wolf for their kill.

Wolverine

Golden eagle

Eagles can have wings that are over two meters (6ft) from tip to tip. Golden eagles hunt over clearings and more open parts of the forest.

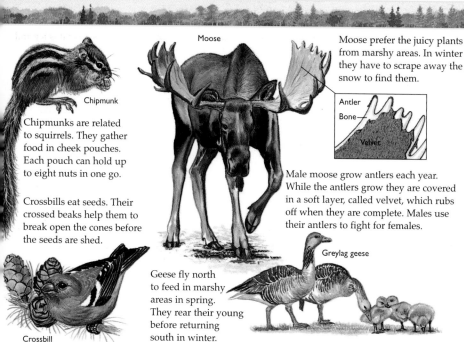

Moose

Moose prefer the juicy plants from marshy areas. In winter they have to scrape away the snow to find them.

Antler
Bone
Velvet

Chipmunk

Chipmunks are related to squirrels. They gather food in cheek pouches. Each pouch can hold up to eight nuts in one go.

Crossbills eat seeds. Their crossed beaks help them to break open the cones before the seeds are shed.

Male moose grow antlers each year. While the antlers grow they are covered in a soft layer, called velvet, which rubs off when they are complete. Males use their antlers to fight for females.

Greylag geese

Geese fly north to feed in marshy areas in spring. They rear their young before returning south in winter.

Crossbill

Peregrine falcons hunt other birds in the air above the trees. They swoop on their prey from above and kill it with a single blow.

Hunting falcon

Rounded wings

European sparrowhawks have rounded wings to help them fly between the tree trunks. They can catch smaller birds and animals in the middle of the forest.

Threatened animals

Most conifer forest animals grow thick coats in winter and many of them used to be hunted for their fur. As they became rare, people also began to hunt more common animals, such as muskrat, skunk and fox. Today some animals are farmed and many others protected.

Sable are closely related to stoats. Their fur was used for many things, including paint brushes. Today few remain in the wild.

Mink are also related to stoats. In the past, farmed mink escaped to the wild. Today, wild mink live close to rivers and marshy areas.

69

Australia's hot, dry forests

The northern part of Australia is tropical, but the south is temperate. Many Australian plants and animals live nowhere else in the world (for more about why, see page 5). Eucalyptus trees are evergreen trees with long, flat leaves. There are about 500 different species of them growing in forests in the south.

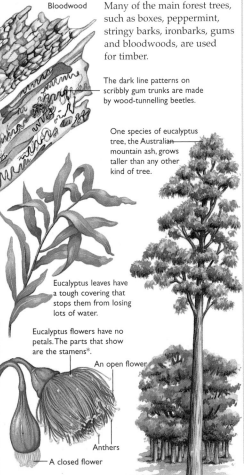

Bloodwood

Many of the main forest trees, such as boxes, peppermint, stringy barks, ironbarks, gums and bloodwoods, are used for timber.

The dark line patterns on scribbly gum trunks are made by wood-tunnelling beetles.

One species of eucalyptus tree, the Australian mountain ash, grows taller than any other kind of tree.

Eucalyptus leaves have a tough covering that stops them from losing lots of water.

Eucalyptus flowers have no petals. The parts that show are the stamens*.

An open flower

Anthers

A closed flower

Life on the ground

Many marsupials* live in the eucalyptus forests. They live the same kind of lives as forest mammals in other parts of the world, but lots of them look very different. Instead of deer, badgers and bears, there are animals such as wallabies, numbats and tasmanian devils.

Numbat

Numbats search among the leaf litter for termites to eat.

Life in the canopy

Because eucalyptus forests are evergreen, there are leaves for food and shelter all year round. Several types of animals spend almost all their lives in the canopy. Animals that do this are called **arboreal** animals. There are also lots of birds that live and feed in the canopy.

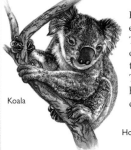

Koalas only eat eucalyptus leaves. They spend most of their lives up trees feeding. Their two thumbs help them grip onto branches.

Koala

Honey possum

Many kinds of possum live in the canopy. The honey possum has a very long tongue and feeds on nectar in flowers. It can steady itself with its strong gripping tail.

*Stamens, 120; Marsupials, 116.

Wallabies and grey kangaroos eat forest plants.

Grey kangaroo

Rabbit bandicoot

Bandicoots, such as rabbit bandicoot, dig under the leaf litter to feed on roots, insects and worms.

Tasmanian devils can open their mouths very wide. They are hunters, with strong necks and heads to help them crunch up bones.

Tasmanian devil

Carpet snake

Many different kinds of parrots feed in the canopy. Some eat wood-tunnelling beetles, like woodpeckers do in other forests.

The red-capped parrot has a finely pointed beak, which helps it to get seeds out of the nuts it eats.

The largest Australian snake is the carpet snake. It is a constrictor* and is not poisonous. It is a good climber and often rests in trees after feeding.

Splendid wren

Kookaburra

The splendid wren is brilliantly colored. It feeds its young on insects.

Kookaburras are like kingfishers. They catch reptiles*, fish and other small mammals.

*Constrictors, 45; Reptiles, 116.   71

Polar regions

The polar regions are at the far north and south of the Earth. They are the Arctic in the north and the Antarctic in the south. They are freezing cold all year. Near the center points (or poles) it rarely snows. These areas are called deserts.

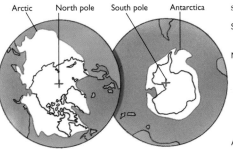

Arctic   North pole   South pole   Antarctica

These are views of the Earth from the top and the bottom.

Polar seasons

Every year the Earth moves gradually around the sun, tilted at an angle. When the northern half of the Earth is tilted towards the sun, it has summer and the south has winter. Because of the Earth's tilt, polar regions have constant daylight in summer and total darkness all winter.

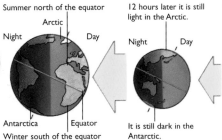

Summer north of the equator
Arctic
Night   Day

12 hours later it is still light in the Arctic.
Night   Day

Antarctica   Equator
Winter south of the equator

It is still dark in the Antarctic.

The Antarctic

The Antarctic is made up of land surrounded by a vast icy ocean. Hardly anything can live on the land because it is always covered with a thick layer of ice. Almost all the animals find their food in the sea, eating plankton*, or animals that have been eating plankton.

Because there is constant light in the summer, the plankton can make food all the time and grow quickly, so there is more food for the animals. Penguins and seals produce their young in the summer when there is lots of food.

The ice on the ocean thaws and breaks up into large lumps called **icebergs** in the summer.

Penguins have flipper-like wings and cannot fly. They spend a lot of time on the ice to avoid hunters such as leopard seals.

Skua   Birds such as gulls and skuas scavenge* and hunt amongst penguin colonies.

*Plankton, 22; Scavengers, 44.

Surviving in the cold

Six months later, the southern half is tilted towards the sun, so it has summer. The northern half now has winter.

Six months later, the Arctic has winter and constant darkness.

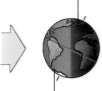

The Antarctic has summer and constant daylight.

Many polar animals are large and rounded, with a thick layer of fat under the skin, to help them keep warm. Whereas desert animals have large ears to lose heat (see page 55), polar animals have small ears to save heat. Hair or feathers trap air around their body which is warmer than the air outside and keeps the animal warm.

Arctic fox

An arctic fox is rounder than a fennec fox (see page 54), with small ears.

Seals have a layer of fat, called **blubber**.

Ptarmigans have feathery legs.

Ptarmigan

Leopard seal

The Arctic

The Arctic is a huge sea of ice, surrounded by the northern parts of America, Europe and Asia. This land is called the **tundra**. In the tundra, summer and winter are very different.

Under the top layer of soil, the ground stays frozen. It is called **permafrost**. This means plants cannot grow long roots. They do not grow very tall because of the strong winds.

In the summer the ice on the tundra melts, plants spring up and animals, such as caribou, arrive from farther south to spend the summer (see page 9). Other animals live in the sea all year.

Many insects live and feed on the bright flowers.

Fireweed

Moss campion

Caribou

Tundra plant-eaters include insects, lemmings and larger animals, such as caribou. The caribou eat reindeer moss.

Plover

Boggy lakes form on the surface because the melted snow cannot soak into the icy ground. Plovers and other birds feed there.

The Antarctic

Mosses and lichens are the only common land plants in the Antarctic. The ocean is rich with plankton*, however, which is the main food for many fish, birds, seals and whales.

Plants

Mosses and lichens are very simple plants. In the Antarctic they live on any bare, wet patches of rock not covered in snow.

Mosses do not need soil to grow. They have tiny root-like things to take in water.

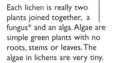

Each lichen is really two plants joined together, a fungus* and an alga. Algae are simple green plants with no roots, stems or leaves. The algae in lichens are very tiny.

Each alga makes its own food, using water which the fungus soaks up, and sunlight. The fungus shares this food as it cannot make its own.

Seals

Seals dive to catch fish and shelled animals, but they have to come up for air. If the ocean is covered in ice they have to scrape a breathing hole in it with their strong front teeth.

Seals have sensitive whiskers to feel objects underwater. Some make high pitched squeaks, like bats (see page 7) and listen for echoes coming off objects.

Antarctic birds

Lots of different sea birds are found in the Antarctic. The most common birds are petrels and penguins.

Penguins have flippers. They use them like wings, to "fly" through the water. They steer with their feet.

To cope with the cold they have a layer of fat under their skin and thousands of tiny feathers all over their bodies.

Chinstrap penguin

Emperor penguins

In an area the size of this box, they have 70 feathers.

The largest penguins, Emperor penguins, live closest to the south pole. It is colder nearer the south pole and their size helps them to keep warm. They mate* on the ice in winter, in the dark, and lay one egg.

74

*Fungi, 65; Mating, 16; Plankton, 22.

The largest seals, elephant seals, can grow to six meters (19ft) long. In spring each male gathers a group of females on the shore to mate*.

Male elephant seal

If another male arrives he rears up and roars with a short trunk on his nose.

The hole in the ozone layer

A layer of ozone gas stops most of the sun's harmful ultra-violet radiation from reaching the Earth. However, gases called CFCs, released from poorly made aerosols and refrigerators, make holes in the ozone layer, letting through extra radiation.

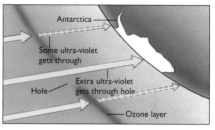

Antarctica

Some ultra-violet gets through

Hole

Extra ultra-violet gets through hole

Ozone layer

There is a huge hole in the ozone layer, over the Antarctic. The extra ulra-violet radiation may give people skin cancer as far away as Australia. It also kills plankton at the surface of the oceans.

Chick on parent's feet

Petrel

Petrels rest on the ocean surface and only go onto land in summer, to lay eggs. If they are attacked, they spit out a jet of stomach oil.

The mother hunts for squid and the young chick takes the food from her mouth. The parents know which chick is theirs by its call.

Male emperor penguins carry the egg on their feet under a fold of skin for two months until it is ready to hatch. During this time they do not eat anything and huddle together in groups of thousands to keep warm.

Penguins feed their young until the summer comes and there is plenty of food around. Then the young learn to hunt for themselves.

Mother feeding chick

75

The Arctic

Some animals live all year around in the Arctic, both in the sea and on the tundra*. Many others visit in summer when the ice melts, forming lakes on the land and breaking up in the sea.

Living in the sea

Seals are found in the Arctic as well as the Antarctic. Walruses are very closely related to seals. They are large and strong and very few animals attack them. They use two long tusks to attack other walruses and haul themselves onto the ice to rest. They have strong lips and suck clams out of their shells to eat. A walrus can eat 3,000 clams in one day.

Summer in the tundra

The plants which spring up in the summer are the main source of food for many animals. For instance, thousands of insects such as beetles, mosquitoes and butterflies feed on them and lay eggs, which hatch the following spring.

Arctic ringlet

Arctic ringlets have dark colors as this helps them to warm up in the sun.

Wader

Many birds, such as swans, divers and waders, travel to the lakes.

Waders have long legs and beaks and poke into the mud for insects and worms.

Swans have broad beaks and long necks to find fish, frogs and shelled animals underwater.

Divers plunge underwater to catch food. They can dive for up to 90 seconds.

Swan

Diver

Wolves

Lots of plant-eating animals means plenty of food for meat-eaters. Wolves hunt in packs (groups). This helps them to wear out stronger musk oxen and faster caribou.

Musk oxen protect their young from wolves inside a ring of adults. They can hook attacking wolves over their shoulders and trample them to death.

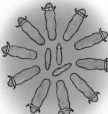

*Tundra, 73.

Polar bears are the biggest and strongest animals in the Arctic and no other animals attack them. They spend most of the year on the ice of the frozen sea, hunting seals.

Polar bear with cubs.

Cubs are born in snow dens in the middle of winter. The mother feeds them with her milk, but cannot eat anything herself until it is warm enough to go out hunting.

For part of the summer, polar bears go onto the land to grow new fur. On land, they eat grass, lichen, bilberries and lemmings.

Polar bears kill seals by grabbing them when they come up for air.

Finding food in winter

In the winter snow, it is hard for plant-eaters to find food. Some, such as caribou, go south, while others, such as lemmings, burrow underground to find plant roots. Other plant-eaters and meat-eaters search for their usual food.

Musk ox

Musk oxen, hares and squirrels look for windy areas where the snow has blown away and scrape the plants out.

Meat-eaters hunt and scavenge* where they can. Stoats chase lemming through their burrows and animals such as foxes scavenge the remains of seals left by polar bears.

Stoat

Musk ox

Wolves look for a young or injured animal to attack. Once they have killed and eaten, the wolves will not attack again until they are hungry.

The wolves hold their heads up when they are not hunting.

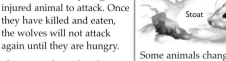
Hunting   Not hunting

Some animals change color during the year, so that their hunters or their prey cannot spot them easily.

Arctic hares are white in winter to blend in with the snow, but grow brown fur in spring to blend in with the grass.

Summer coat   Winter coat

Mountains

Mountains cover 5% of the land's surface. They were formed over millions of years by movements in the Earth's crust (see page 4). The higher up you go, the colder, drier and windier it gets. There is also less oxygen in the air and the soil is very poor. Few plants and animals can live at the very top of mountains.

Mountain bands

As you go down a mountain, there are more and more plants. There are also bands of different types of plant as you go down. This is because the conditions for survival get easier and more types of plants can survive at each new level.

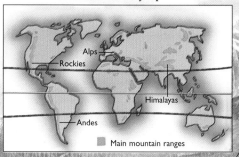

Alps
Rockies
Himalayas
Andes

Main mountain ranges

The Alps are a large range of mountains in Europe.

The top of a mountain is covered in ice and snow and nothing can grow.

Even though there are no plants, some insects and spiders can live at the very top. This is because they eat pollen, seeds and tiny, dead insects blown up from the valleys by the winds.

A phalangid spider can lower its body into hollows in the snow to reach dead insects which have sunk down in it.

Below the snow peaks is an area similar to the Arctic tundra*. Only mosses and lichens grow here and only a few animals can survive. Lower down, this merges into a band of shrubs and grasses, where more animals can survive.

Golden eagles scavenge and hunt.

Chamois

Alpine marmots eat plants. They hibernate* for over half a year in deep grass-lined burrows.

Marmot

The point at which trees begin to appear is called the **timberline**. Below it, the soil is good enough for them to grow and the conditions are less cold and harsh. At the timberline itself, the trees are shaped by the strong winds into weird, stunted shapes.

African mountains

The bands of plants and animals found going down a mountain vary in different parts of the world. Mount Kenya in Africa is almost on the equator. Like other tropical mountains, it has different bands of plants on it from those on temperate mountains.

Evergreen* forest grows in a band where the air is cold and dry and a variety of animals live here. Many birds live in the trees, eating the seeds and the insects living on the trunks.

Pine marten

Crossbill

At the bottom there is a band of deciduous* forest. It is not too cold and many animals live and feed here throughout the year.

Red fox

Black grouse

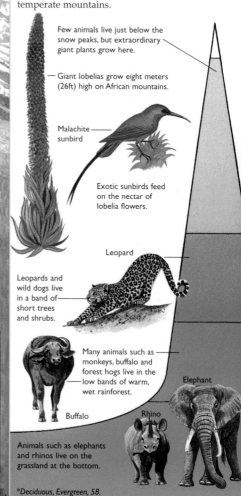

Few animals live just below the snow peaks, but extraordinary giant plants grow here.

Giant lobelias grow eight meters (26ft) high on African mountains.

Malachite sunbird

Exotic sunbirds feed on the nectar of lobelia flowers.

Leopard

Leopards and wild dogs live in a band of short trees and shrubs.

Many animals such as monkeys, buffalo and forest hogs live in the low bands of warm, wet rainforest.

Buffalo

Elephant

Rhino

Animals such as elephants and rhinos live on the grassland at the bottom.

*Deciduous, Evergreen, 58.

Living in a mountain climate

The high mountain climate is very harsh, and plants and animals living there have to cope with the smaller amount of oxygen and the cold, dry, windy conditions.

Using oxygen

Animals need the gas oxygen from their surroundings. They use it in their bodies to get energy from their food. This process produces another gas, carbon dioxide.

Tiny animals can get oxygen from air or water to their whole body through their skin.

Larger animals have a special system, the **blood system**, to carry oxygen all around their bodies.

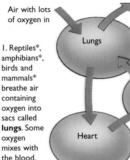

Air with lots of oxygen in

Air with more carbon dioxide out

Lungs

1. Reptiles*, amphibians*, birds and mammals* breathe air containing oxygen into sacs called **lungs**. Some oxygen mixes with the blood.

Heart

5. The animal breathes carbon dioxide out into the air.

4. Carbon dioxide is carried back to the lungs in the blood.

Rest of body

3. The oxygen is used up in the body and carbon dioxide is produced.

2. The blood is pushed around the body in tubes by a pump called the **heart**.

Coping with the cold

Animals in high mountain regions cope with the cold in similar ways to polar animals (see page 73). They are often large and fat, with thick hair or feathers covering them. Many are less active and produce young less often than their relatives in other places. High mountain plants tend to grow very slowly.

Himalayan lichen

Some lichens at the tops of mountains may only be able to grow for one day each year, because it is so cold.

Some humming birds live high up mountains eating flower nectar. They hover by beating their wings very quickly, using up lots of energy.

Yak

Yaks live in Tibet and China. Their thick coats protect them from freezing temperatures.

— Streamertail

To save heat, they often let their body get colder and go into a deep rest called **torpor**.

80

Amphibians, Mammals, Reptiles, 116.

Because the air around them has less oxygen in it, many mountain animals, such as llamas, have blood which can take in more oxygen with each breath. They breathe more quickly as well.

Coping with strong winds

Mountain winds are often very strong. Plants high up often grow in low clumps, to avoid being blown away or dried out by the wind. They have long roots to hold them in the ground. Mountain birds have to be very strong to fly against the wind, so most small birds and insects that live high up never fly.

Llama

Plants such as gentian grow in short, round clumps on mountains.

Gentian

Lammergeiers are strong, fast-flying birds which live high up mountains.

Mountain grass seeds grow roots and shoots before they are shed from the parent plant, to give them a good start in the poor soil.

Mountain grass

Lammergeier

Their talons (huge claws) are strong enough to lift large bones into the air. They drop them from a height to shatter them so they can eat the center part, or **marrow**.

Alpine salamander

Eurasian wallcreeper

Eurasian wallcreepers run up and down cliffs with long, sharp claws, using their tail for support. They look for insects in cracks in the rocks.

Most salamanders lay eggs. On mountains it is too cold for eggs to hatch, so mountain kinds give birth to live young.

Springtails use a spring at the back of their body to jump along.

Springtail

Spring

81

An isolated life

Mountain ranges may be separated from each other by huge distances, but animals which live high up on mountains are often similar because they have to cope with similar problems.

Similar habits

Above the timberline*, winters are harsh. Small plants are covered up by the snow. Around the world, the few plant-eaters which live high up cope with this in similar ways. Many travel down the mountain in winter searching for food. Others collect and store food in advance. The very few meat-eaters which survive high up also have similar ways of life.

Chamois from Europe and Asia are good climbers. They live in herds. One of the herd looks out for danger, and whistles and stamps to warn the others. In winter they feed low down on pine shoots and moss.

Chamois

Rocky mountain goat

Rocky mountain goats in North America are closely related to chamois. Their small hoofs help them to climb steep rocks to escape hunters.

Ibexes live high up in European, African and Asian mountains, eating grass and lichen. The adults leave their young hidden in holes in the rocks when they have to travel down the mountain to find food. Pads on the back of their feet help them climb steep rocks.

Ibex

Vicuña

Vicuñas live in groups high up in the Andes. They spit strong smelling liquid and chewed food at attackers. Their hoofs are sharp, with a thick sole and a curved part which grips rock firmly.

*Timberline, 78.

Rare animals

Many mountain animals can only find their food in one area on a mountain. Because they cannot feed higher up or lower down, they are easily upset by changes to their surroundings. This is why many, such as bears and gorillas, are rare.

Spectacled bear

Mountain gorillas that live in the forests low down on African mountains are rare because so much forest has been cut down.

Mountain gorilla

Desman

Desmans find food in fast-flowing mountain streams in Europe. Building dams there removes this food source.

Spectacled bears live and feed in forests in the Andes. They are rare because many forest areas where they live and find their food have been cut down.

Snow leopard

Himalayan snow leopards travel long distances in the day to hunt sheep, small mammals and birds. At night they shelter in dens.

Puma

Pumas in American mountains hunt mammals such as sheep by day. They hide extra food to eat later. Most other pumas hunt at night.

Alpine chough

Pika

Pikas in North America and Asia store dried leaves in hollows for the winter.

Alpine choughs from Europe, Asia and North Africa eat worms and insects, storing spare food in cracks in rocks.

83

Rivers and lakes

Water is continually recycled in nature in the water cycle*. Unlike sea water, the rain, snow and hail which falls from clouds has no salt in it. It is called fresh water. When it falls on land some of it soaks in, but most drains off into streams and rivers, which flow to the sea. As they flow, they collect silt (tiny bits of rocks and plants) and the water gets murkier.

The path of a river

Different kinds of plants and animals live in different parts of a river. The river shown here would be found in a temperate area.

In fast-flowing streams, most plants are washed away. Only slim, strong fish such as salmon can live here.

Stonefly larvae* have a flat body and cling on to stones with strong claws.

Salmon

In valleys the water flows more slowly and more plants grow. Fish such as minnows and grayling feed and rest here.

Minnow

Grayling

Water crowfoot

How do rivers and lakes form?

Water can soak through some rock, called **permeable rock**, but not other rock, called **impermeable rock**.

Where permeable rock lies at the surface, some water from rain or melted ice soaks down until it reaches impermeable rock, where it stops and collects in a layer.

Permeable rock

Impermeable rock

Many more kinds of plants and fish are found lower down the river, in wide bends where the water is shallow and slow-moving.

Tench have narrow bodies and weave in and out of underwater leaves.

Arrowhead

Barbels detect objects in the underwater gloom with sensitive "whiskers".

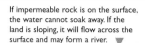

If impermeable rock is on the surface, the water cannot soak away. If the land is sloping, it will flow across the surface and may form a river. ▼

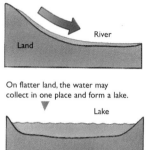

Land
River

On flatter land, the water may collect in one place and form a lake. ▼

Land
Lake

Most rivers start on high, sloping ground. The slope makes most of the water move downwards in a small, fast-flowing stream, even if the rock at the surface is permeable.

As the land flattens out and other streams join, the river flows more and more slowly. This gives more time for water to soak into permeable rocks. If the rocks fill up, the water cannot soak away and marshy areas form.

If there is impermeable rock on the surface, a lake may form, because the river "spreads out" over the land. The river flows on through the lake.

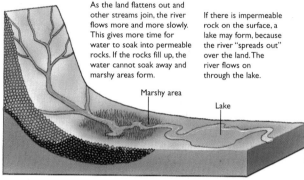

Marshy area

Lake

Many birds and mammals live on the banks of slow-moving rivers and lakes. They feed on fish, plants and tiny animals in the water.

Lots of plants grow around lakes. They are home to many fish, frogs, insects and other animals.

Water vole

Pond skaters are so light, they can walk on the surface film of the water. They eat tiny dead animals and bits of plants falling on it.

Duckweed floats in a mass on open water. Each leaf has one root.

Some insect larvae, such as those of dragonflies, live on the muddy bottom of lakes. Many change into adults which only live in the air.

Kingfisher

Emperor dragonfly

Dragonfly larvae

Getting oxygen underwater

All animals need oxygen to help them get energy from their food. Most fish and many other water-living animals get their oxygen from the water, instead of from the air. They have special parts called gills which they use to do this.

How gills work

Gills are thin and feathery. Many animals, such as fish, have them inside their bodies, under a flap, or **gill cover**, but others, especially young forms such as tadpoles, have them sticking out from the sides of their heads.

The fish "breathes" in water through its mouth.

Gill cover

The fish "breathes" out water from behind its gill cover.

Gills (gill cover has been removed in this diagram)

Oxygen from the water passes into the blood in the gills and is carried around the body.

Carbon dioxide produced in the body is carried back to the gills in the blood and passes into the water.

Young tadpoles have external gills growing from their head.

These gills are later replaced by covered gills.

Other ways of getting oxygen

Many insects and larger animals such as frogs and some fish, spend part of their lives on land and part in water. Some of these live on land but feed in water. Others hatch and live in water in their young form, but come onto land as adults. They get oxygen in different ways.

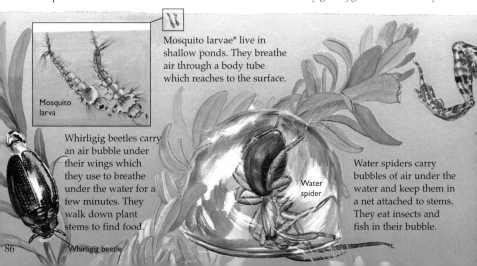

Mosquito larvae* live in shallow ponds. They breathe air through a body tube which reaches to the surface.

Mosquito larva

Whirligig beetles carry an air bubble under their wings which they use to breathe under the water for a few minutes. They walk down plant stems to find food.

Water spider

Water spiders carry bubbles of air under the water and keep them in a net attached to stems. They eat insects and fish in their bubble.

Whirligig beetle

Pollution in rivers and lakes

Acid rain from air pollution (see page 67) makes the water in rivers and lakes acid. Few plants can grow in acid water and animals die because the acid stops oxygen from getting into the blood in their gills. Acid lakes and rivers look crystal clear, as hardly anything can live in them.

Dippers used to be common in England, but they are rarer now. The larvae they used to eat have died because of river water turning to acid.

Sometimes fertilizers containing nitrates* wash into rivers and lakes from farmland. The nitrates provide lots of food for fresh water algae* so they can grow quickly. However, at night, they use up oxygen instead of producing it (see page 6). They get this from the water.

If there are too many algae, the oxygen supply in the water gets used up, so there is not enough for fish and other animals. Many of them die. The water looks green and sludgy with algae.

If their pond dries up, South American armored catfish can survive for up to four hours by gulping air. They move across wet mud to find water.

Armored catfish

Frog

Though tadpoles have gills, adult frogs have lungs and breathe air, but they can also take oxygen through their skins from air and water.

They have strong spines on two of their fins. They use these to support themselves and move by wriggling from side to side.

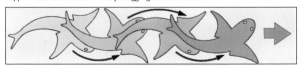

Lungfish live in lakes and rivers which sometimes dry up. They have lungs as well as gills, so they can take oxygen from air as well as from water.

African lungfish can survive for months or years without water, resting in the slimy mud of a dried-up river.

*Algae, 116; Larvae, 17; Nitrates, 13.

87

Fresh water plants and animals

Most water plants grow in slow moving or still water, in the later stages of rivers and lakes. Many animals find their food and lay their eggs among the plants.

Plants

Some plants rooted in a river or lake bed have leaves above water. Others with underwater leaves grow in shallow water where enough sunlight gets through. They all have ways of coping with life in water.

Water crowfoot

Water crowfoot has long, thin leaves under the water. This stops the water currents from pulling them off.

Water lily

Water lily leaves and flowers float on the surface. The leaves are waxy so water runs off.

Spiked water milfoil has all its leaves underwater, but its flowers grow above the surface where they are pollinated*.

Hornwort

Spiked water milfoil

Hornwort grows completely under the water. To pollinate* a female flower, a male flower floats to the surface. Its pollen sinks down, falling on the female part.

Protecting eggs and young

Most female amphibians* and fish lay many eggs in water. The male sheds sperm* over the eggs to fertilize* them, but most drift away before this, or get eaten because they are left unguarded. Only some adults protect their eggs and young.

Cichlid

Some cichlids hold their eggs in their mouth. Their young also dart into their mouth, to avoid danger.

Food for fish

There are thousands of different types of fresh water fish in lakes and rivers around the world. Most eat plankton (tiny plants and animals).

Young bream eat plankton, but the adults feed mainly on insect larvae*, worms and shelled animals.

Adult bream

Paddlefish

Paddlefish have a long paddle-shaped snout which they use to stir up the muddy bottom. They filter out plankton to eat.

Some female newts attach their eggs to underwater plants. They fold leaves over to hide them.

Female newt

Male Surinam toads push their eggs into the female's back. The skin covers them until they have hatched and grown into frogs.

Male Surinam toad

Male midwife toads carry their eggs safely wound around their legs until they are nearly ready to hatch.

Male midwife toad

Reptiles* lay eggs that are already fertilized. They lay fewer eggs than amphibians and fish. The eggs are laid on land and have a shell to stop them from drying out. Only a few reptiles guard their eggs and many eggs get eaten.

Female South American tartarugas gather to lay their eggs in the sand. When the young hatch, they burrow out and run to the river.

Newly-hatched tartarugas

Female North American alligator on a nest

Female North American alligators guard their eggs in nests built out of plants and mud. The young grunt when they hatch, which tells the mother to open the nest. She protects her young for up to three years.

Pike often hide among plants to catch fish and small animals. They are fast-swimming hunters, with slim bodies and sharp, slanting teeth.

Pike

Lampreys have a sucker-like mouth, with sharp teeth. They cling to other fish, scrape through their skin and eat their blood and flesh.

Sucker-like mouth

Lampreys

*Reptiles, 116.

Living by rivers and lakes

As well as amphibians such as frogs and toads, many mammals live by rivers and lakes. Some are well shaped for swimming and hunt underwater. Others dive in to cool down or hide from hunters.

Swimming mammals

Many mammals have flat tails and skin between their toes, making them like paddles. These are called **webbed feet**. They help them to push through the water.

Platypuses are mammals that lay eggs. They swim well and hunt for food such as shrimps under the water.

Platypus

Males can defend themselves with poisonous spines on their back feet.

Their webbed feet are flipper-like because the flaps of skin come out a long way past their claws. The skin folds away when they walk on land.

Platypuses have flaps of skin to protect their eyes and ears in water. They use their sensitive snout to detect prey.

Otters

Otters are energetic, playful animals. Mother otters teach their young to hunt in water by giving them half-dead animals, such as fish, frogs and turtles, so they can practice diving and swooping to catch their prey.

Beavers live in forests in Northern Europe and North America. They build dams out of sticks across small rivers to make lakes. Here they build their homes, called lodges, where they live in family groups of up to 12 beavers.

Beaver

Beavers use their huge front teeth to chop down trees. They eat the shoots and use the sticks for building. They carry logs in their mouths.

They have webbed back feet and large flat tails to help them move easily in the water.

Water opossums dive to catch fish, frogs and shelled animals. They are marsupials*. The females' pouches close tightly so the young do not drown.

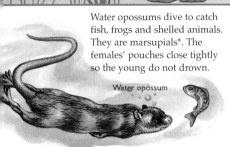

Water opossum

Coypus can stay underwater for five minutes, finding plants and shelled animals to eat.

Coypu

They have webbed hind feet and produce a special liquid to make their fur waterproof. Females carry their young above the water.

Water shrew

Water shrews chase prey underwater, killing them with a poisonous bite. They have flat tail and paddle with fringed toes.

Tapirs live near water in dense tropical forests. They have a short, sensitive trunk-like nose to reach out for leaves and shoots.

Malayan tapirs swim expertly to find water plants and escape hunters. The bands of color on their skin blend in with the shadows so it is hard for hunters to see them.

Meat-eating plants

Soil near water is usually rich in nitrates*, but in some marshy areas it is very poor. Few plants can live in these areas, but some special ones can get nitrates from dead, rotting insects. They produce liquids to make them rot faster.

Sundew leaves have tentacles which insects stick to while the leaf rolls over them.

Venus flytrap leaves have stiff spines and are hinged. When an insect touches sensitive hairs, the leaves snap shut, trapping them.

Pitcher plants have hollow, tube-like leaves. They make a sweet-smelling nectar which attracts insects into the tube.

Downward pointing, sticky hairs inside the tube stop insects from climbing out again. They fall to the bottom and rot in the liquid made by the plant. The plant takes in the liquid.

*Marsupials, 116; Nitrates, 13.

Water birds

Many water birds live around lakes, rivers and wetlands, where there is plenty of food for them. Many dive to find their food. Their feathers are waterproof and make their body a smooth shape, good for swimming or flying.

Feeding

Many water birds have specially shaped bodies, feet and beaks to help them find food in a particular way.

Kingfishers have a short body with a long beak and strong wings. They dart into the water from a perch to grab a fish.

Feathers

Many adult birds have fluffy **down feathers** on their body which help to keep them warm. These lie under other, stronger feathers which cover them in a smooth, waterproof layer.

Each covering feather is made up of hundreds of strands, or **barbs**, coming off a central **shaft**. The bird makes a special oil near its tail and spreads this over the feathers with its beak to make water run off.

Shaft
Barb
Barbule

Each barb has lots of **barbules** which hook together to keep the feather in shape. When a bird preens its feathers it is "zipping up" any barbs that are unhooked.

Grey heron

Jacanas, or lily trotters, have long toes and walk on lily leaves, looking for insects to eat. They step onto the next leaf before the one they are standing on sinks.

Many birds, such as herons, have long legs and stand still or wade in shallow water, waiting to grab fish or frogs.

Jacana

Tropical skimmer

Tropical skimmers fly low over water, skimming fish and shrimps from the surface with long beaks. The lower part of their beaks is longer than the top part.

Birds such as pelicans swim on the surface. The lower part of their beak forms a pouch, which they use to scoop up lots of fish.

Pelican

Attracting a mate

All animals try to attract a mate. This is called **courtship**. Different birds have different ways of courting a mate, such as singing, showing off special feathers or moving about in a pattern or dance.

Crane

Cranes clatter their beaks and hop up and down in a complicated dance.

When a great crested grebe sees a possible mate, it dives and comes up near it.

The courting grebe swim towards each other, shaking their heads from side to side.

They then dive down and come up breast to breast with weed in their beaks.

Grebe

Flamingo

Shoebills have a thick beak and dig lungfish out of the mud. They also wait quietly to pounce on fish and frogs.

Spoonbills and flamingos swing their heads from side to side in water or mud, filtering out food.

Shoebill

Flamingos have wide feet so they do not sink into the mud as they feed.

They nest in huge groups. Each female lays one egg. It hatches after about 28 days.

Roseate spoonbill

The Amazon

The Amazon river is a tropical river in South America. It is the largest river in the world, covering thousands of miles. By the time it reaches the sea it is very muddy, because it has picked up so much silt*. Because of the hot, wet tropical conditions, an amazing variety of plants and animals live in and around the Amazon river.

Giants

Because it is hot and there is plenty of water and food, Amazon plants and animals often grow to giant sizes.

Capybaras are the largest rodents* in the world. They are gentle animals, living in family groups and eating water plants.

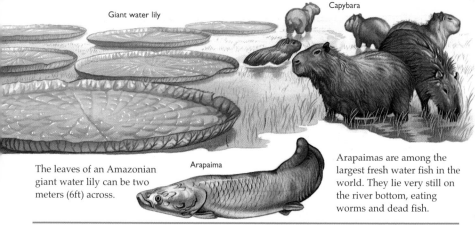

Giant water lily

Capybara

Arapaima

The leaves of an Amazonian giant water lily can be two meters (6ft) across.

Arapaimas are among the largest fresh water fish in the world. They lie very still on the river bottom, eating worms and dead fish.

Moving around underwater

Because the Amazon is so muddy, it is hard for animals to see and some have special ways to work out where they are and detect their prey.

Fresh water river dolphins, like bats (see page 7), make high-pitched sounds and listen for the echoes coming back off objects such as fish and shelled animals (their food).

Some fish, such as electric eels, produce electricity which they use to find and stun their prey. They can produce an electric shock strong enough to stun even a horse.

Electric eel

Dolphin

Matamata turtles lie in wait on the river bottom. When they feel ripples as small fish swim by, they open their jaws and their prey is sucked in.

Matamata turtle

*Rodents, 48; Silt, 32.

Hunters

Because there is so much animal life, many hunters live in and around the Amazon river, taking advantage of the plentiful supply of food.

Piranhas have strong jaws, with extremely sharp triangular teeth.

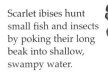

Piranha

Scarlet ibis

Scarlet ibises hunt small fish and insects by poking their long beak into shallow, swampy water.

Caiman

Anaconda

Caimans are related to crocodiles. They hide underwater, breathing air with nostrils on top of their head. They thrash through water with their strong tail, catching birds, mammals* and fish.

Anacondas are among the largest snakes in the world. They grow to about eight meters (26ft) long. They attack caimans, mammals and birds and suffocate them by squeezing them.

Fish-eating bat

Fish-eating bats look for any fish that ripple the water surface. They swoop and grab their prey with clawed feet.

Poisonous animals

Because there are so many hunters in the Amazon, many animals have special ways to protect themselves. Some of them use poison.

Arrow poison frog

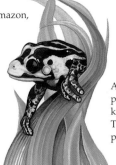

Freshwater stingrays have long tails with poisonous spines that stick into any animal that touches them.

Freshwater stingray

Arrow poison frogs have poison in their skin which kills animals that bite them. Their bright colors warn off predators (see page 109).

* Mammals, 116.

Tropical rainforests

Hot tropical forests grow between the tropic lines (see page 8). In some tropical areas there are wet and dry seasons and the forest trees rest in the dry season. In other tropical areas, though, it is always wet, with rain every day and this is where rainforests grow.

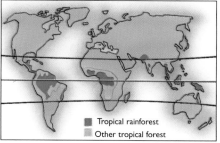

Tropical rainforest

Other tropical forest

Rainforest trees

There are hundreds of different types of trees in rainforests. Many grow up to 45m (150ft) tall. The trees are evergreen* because, since it is always hot and wet, they can keep their leaves and continue growing all year.

Most of the trees quickly grow very tall, with their branches spread out wide at the top, in a race to get enough light. If they were shaded from the light by other trees they would die.

Some trees cannot grow so tall. They survive if they catch enough light through gaps in the trees above. Many of these trees are pointed in shape.

Many tall trees have wide roots, called **buttress roots**, above the ground to support their trunks in the thin soil.

Rainforest life

Rainforests are home to an enormous variety of plants and animals. Most animals live in the tree tops (the canopy) among the fruit and flowers.

The rainforest in South East Asia is probably the tallest in the world.

Animals living in the canopy have to be good at climbing. Orangutans have long toes which help them to grip. They eat fruit and leaves.

To avoid being drenched by heavy rain, many leaves are large and shiny and end in a point called a drip tip. This lets the water drain off.

Brightly-colored orchids grow in the rainforest.

* Evergreen 58.

There is always fruit in the canopy. Some animals hardly eat anything else.

Fruit bats crush fruit on ridges in their mouth. They drink the juice and spit the rest out.

Hornbills have a long, strong beak to push through the leaves and reach fruit.

The constant temperature suits cold-blooded* animals. Snakes such as Wagler's pit vipers hang from branches, waiting to strike prey.

Climbing plants, such as lianas hang in loops between the tops of trees.

Some big birds, such as the Philippine eagle, fly above the tree tops. There is not room for them to open their wings in the canopy.

Many butterflies and other insects live in the canopy.

To move easily between plants on the ground, animals need to be small, with no parts sticking out. Indian elephants live in rain forests. They have quite small ears.

Barbirusas eat plants, insect larvae* and dead animals.

*Cold-blooded, 54; Larvae, 17.

Rainforest plants

The thick, tangled canopies of the tall rainforest trees form an umbrella which shades the ground. Below the canopy it is still, hot and damp, but many plants grow very well there.

Plants living on plants

Some plants can survive in the shade, but many grow higher up, on the trees, so they get more light.

Small plants, such as small palm trees and some grasses, grow in shade.

Palm

Liana

Lianas need light and space to grow. They climb up trees and hang in loops with stems like thick ropes. They do not harm the trees they grow on.

Many kinds of orchids grow on sunny branches. Their roots do not reach the ground, so they store rain-water in fleshy stems and leaves. They get nitrates* from bits of rotting plant in cracks in the tree.

Bromeliad

Orchid

Some plants that grow on trees, such as bromeliads, have leaves arranged in a cup shape. Water and bits of dead, rotting plant collect in the cup. Insects and tiny frogs live in these "mini pools".

Strangler fig

Sometimes one plant or animal, called a parasite*, takes all its food from another plant or animal. Rafflesia is a plant parasite which takes its water and sugars from liana roots.

Rafflesia

Strangler figs grow when their seeds get stuck between branches of trees. They grow roots which reach down to the soil, twining round the tree.

They grow so big that the tree is shaded out. It dies and rots away, leaving the fig standing.

*Nitrates, 13; Parasite, 112.

Flowers and fruit

Many trees grow their flowers and fruit below the flat tangle of branches at the very top. This means they can be reached more easily by insects and other animals which pollinate* the flowers and scatter the fruit seeds as they feed.

Unripe banana fruit

Banana flower

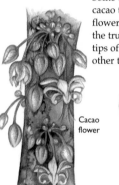

Some trees, such as cacao trees, grow their flowers straight out of the trunk, not on the tips of branches like other trees.

Cacao flower

The fleshy cacao fruit, called **pods**, develop from the flowers on the trunk. The seeds or beans, are used to make chocolate.

Cacao pod

Some trees grow long stalks so their flowers and fruits hang down below the canopy.

Why plants must be saved

Huge areas of rainforest are cut down every day. This destroys the homes of many animals and makes many rare species of plants extinct*. Many of these plants provide people with food and medicine. Others may also be useful, but are cut down before scientists have time to find out.

Many plants, such as rosy periwinkles, are used to make drugs to treat serious diseases.

Rosy periwinkle

Many kinds of exotic fruits grow in rain forests.

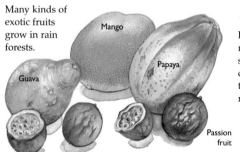

Mango

Papaya

Guava

Passion fruit

Rubber is used to make many things, such as tires. It comes from rubber trees which grow in rain forests.

Man collecting rubber from rubber tree

*Extinctions, 18; Pollination, 14.

The rainforest floor

There is always lots of leaf litter (dead leaves and other bits of plants) falling to the rainforest floor, because the trees are always losing some leaves. All these dead bits of plants, and animals too, rot very quickly (for more about rotting, see page 65). The nitrates* which come from rotting are quickly taken out of the soil by all the living plants which need them.

Tiny animals

Huge numbers of insects live on the forest floor, many of which eat up the leaf litter.

Malayan pill millipede

Malayan pill millipedes eat rotting plants. When frightened, they squirt nasty liquids from their body and curl into a ball.

Termite nest

Termites eat dead wood helping it to rot. Some make nests out of chewed up wood and saliva. These often have wide roofs to keep out rain.

Leaf cutter ants bite leaves from trees and chew them until they are soft and fungus* grows on them. The ants eat the fungus.

Leaf cutter ant

Insect eaters

Because there are so many insects on the forest floor, many larger animals feed on them.

Australian spiny anteaters feed on ants and termites, licking them out of their nests with long, sticky tongues. They roll into a prickly ball when scared.

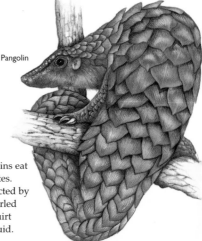
Pangolin

Spiny anteater

African pangolins eat ants and termites. They are protected by scales when curled up and can squirt out a nasty liquid.

Army ants kill any insects or smaller mammals* they find. They move on when there is no food left in an area.

Army ant

Giant centipedes can be 30cm (12in) long. They catch and kill their prey with poisonous claws.

Giant centipede

Cutting down rainforests

Most of the nitrates in rain forests are inside the plants and animals as the plant roots take them from the ground so quickly. This means they are lost if the plants are cut down and removed.

Huge areas of rainforest are cut down every day by people who need land to grow crops. After two or three years the few nitrates in the soil are used up.

No crops will grow and without roots to bind it the soil gets washed away. The people cannot afford fertilizers, so they move to a new area, cut down the trees and start again.

Today, logging companies are destroying more rain forest to build roads. The roads mean more people can enter the forest and clear more trees for crops.

Mantises are large insects with long spiny front legs which they fold up or shoot forward to grab smaller insects.

Mantis

Spiny leg

Aye aye

Skinny finger

Sun bear

Asian sun bears are the smallest bears. They eat ants, plants and honey. They put a paw into ants' nests and lick up the ants.

Aye ayes listen for wood-tunnelling insect larvae* in fallen branches and bite a hole. They use their long, skinny middle finger to scrape them out.

*Larvae, 17; Mammals, 116.

101

Climbing and gliding

Because most of the food is up in the canopy, most animals in rainforests can climb trees and are good at clinging on and jumping about among the branches. This also helps them to escape from hunters. Some are so good at living in the trees that they hardly ever come down.

Clinging on

Many animals have special body parts for climbing, such as strong, clinging tails, called **prehensile tails**, which they use like an extra arm or leg to grip the tree. Some have extra strong fingers and thumbs to help them grip.

Asian tarsiers have "suckers" on their long fingers and toes, to help them grip. They hunt small animals, balancing with their long tails as they leap.

Tarsier

Potto

South American kinkajous have a prehensile tail as long as their body. They live in trees, eating plants, honey and small animals.

Kinkajou

Pottos, from Africa, have thumbs which move in the opposite direction to their fingers, like ours, and a short first finger. This gives them a very strong grip. They eat insects, birds and fruit.

Sloths spend almost all their lives in trees and can hardly move on the ground. Some feed only on one kind of tree leaf.

Sloth

They move very slowly, chewing leaves and fruit, hanging upside down by hook-like claws. Their fur hangs from their belly to their back, so rain runs off.

Emerald tree boa

South American emerald tree boas coil over a branch. They uncoil to catch prey and hang on by the last coil.

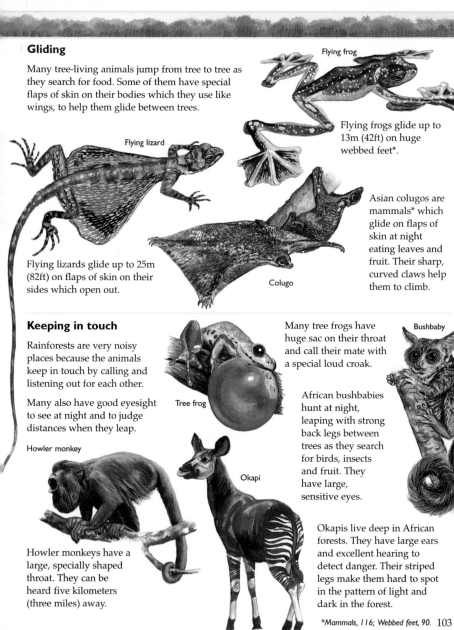

Gliding

Many tree-living animals jump from tree to tree as they search for food. Some of them have special flaps of skin on their bodies which they use like wings, to help them glide between trees.

Flying frog

Flying frogs glide up to 13m (42ft) on huge webbed feet*.

Flying lizard

Asian colugos are mammals* which glide on flaps of skin at night eating leaves and fruit. Their sharp, curved claws help them to climb.

Flying lizards glide up to 25m (82ft) on flaps of skin on their sides which open out.

Colugo

Keeping in touch

Rainforests are very noisy places because the animals keep in touch by calling and listening out for each other.

Many also have good eyesight to see at night and to judge distances when they leap.

Tree frog

Many tree frogs have huge sac on their throat and call their mate with a special loud croak.

Bushbaby

African bushbabies hunt at night, leaping with strong back legs between trees as they search for birds, insects and fruit. They have large, sensitive eyes.

Howler monkey

Okapi

Howler monkeys have a large, specially shaped throat. They can be heard five kilometers (three miles) away.

Okapis live deep in African forests. They have large ears and excellent hearing to detect danger. Their striped legs make them hard to spot in the pattern of light and dark in the forest.

*Mammals, 116; Webbed feet, 90. 103

Monkeys and apes

Many monkeys and apes live in rainforests. They are related to people and come from a group of animals called primates. Most primates have grasping, sensitive fingers and thumbs, long arms and legs, good eyesight, and a big brain for the size of their body.

Different kinds of primates

Apes have very long arms. They do not have a tail and are the closest relatives of people. Monkeys have tails and most climb about high up in the trees. They feed on plant food during the day. Other primates, such as lorises, usually sleep during the day and come out at night and many of them are insect-eaters.

Slow loris

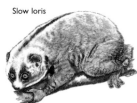

Asian slow lorises quietly climb through the trees at night, eating small animals, fruit and insects.

Gorilla

Gorillas are the biggest apes. They are too big and heavy to climb easily and they spend most of the time walking on the ground on all fours.

The male leader of a group of gorillas has a silver-gray back. When other groups come near, he hoots, throws branches, beats his chest and hits the ground.

South American monkeys look different from other monkeys. Their nostrils point sideways instead of downwards.

Uakaris are monkeys from South America.

Mandrills are monkeys from Africa.

Moving about in the trees

Most primates are at home in the trees, climbing and jumping about easily, looking for food.

Squirrel monkeys can leap long distances between trees, carrying their young on their backs.

Spider monkeys

Adult spider monkeys sometimes make a bridge for their young to climb across.

Gibbons are apes. They swing from branch to branch at amazing speeds using strong fingers and very long thumbs.

Gibbon

Squirrel monkeys

Living together

Most primates live in groups and defend their home area against other groups.

A male black and white colobus monkey guards a group of 9 to 13 females and young. He stares at other groups, clicks his tongue and shakes branches at them.

Black and white colobus monkeys

Douroucoulis are the only monkeys to come out at night. Their large eyes help them see in the dark. They live in pairs, high up in the trees. The males hit other monkeys which come near them.

Douroucoulis

Marmosets

Marmosets have claws to help them climb. To attract a mate, a male curves his back, smacks his lips and sticks out his tongue. Each male lives with his mate and young. Like many primates, marmosets lick the fur of others in their group and "comb" it with their teeth. This is called **grooming**.

Chimpanzees are apes. They climb easily and run on all fours. They hoot loudly when they gather for a feast or when the males show off to decide who will be leader.

Chimpanzees hooting

Chimpanzees make nests in the trees.

Chimpanzee young stay with their mother for about six years. They play together, groom each other and even hold hands.

Chimpanzees use sticks and stones as tools. They catch termites on twigs which they prod into termite nests.

105

Rain forest hunters

The huge number of plant-eating animals in rain forests means there is lots of food for hunters. Most hunt at night, when it is easier for them to surprise their prey and make a kill. They usually have very good eyesight and hearing and a good sense of smell.

Cats

Rain forest cats hunt alone. Big cats, such as tigers, hunt animals bigger than themselves, to last them several meals. Cats are slim, with long tails and strong, sharp claws which fold away when they are walking, to keep them sharp. Their stripes or spots help them to blend in with the patterns of light coming through leaves.

Tigers come from Asia. They hunt deer, pigs, buffaloes and smaller animals. They knock prey down from behind and kill them with a bite in the neck. They cut meat with their teeth and swallow it in lumps.

Tiger

Young tigers playing

Young tigers and leopards learn to hunt with their mothers, by creeping up on prey and killing it after their mother has caught it. They also learn to hunt by playing.

Leopard

Leopards creep up and jump on their prey. They can run, swim and climb, balancing with their long tails. They kill prey by breaking their necks.

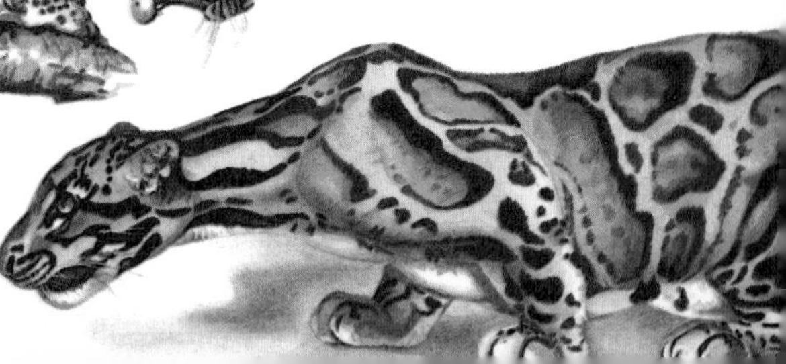

South American jaguars follow groups of animals, such as deer and attack any that lag behind. They also attack animals that come to drink at rivers.

Jaguar

Other hunters

There are lots of other rain forest hunters. Many of them come out at night.

Tayras can climb easily and run very fast. They hunt at night for birds and small mammals.

Vampire bat

Tayra

Vampire bats make thin slits with sharp teeth in the flesh of sleeping animals, without waking them. They lick up the blood with their long tongues.

Ocelots are small South American cats. They hunt small mammals* and birds on the ground and can also climb easily.

Ocelot

Harpy eagles hunt monkeys, sloths, coatis and small mammals, birds and snakes, killing them with sharp claws. The young practice by grasping dead animals in their claws.

Harpy eagle

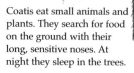

Clouded leopards are small cats. They climb trees and catch monkeys, small mammals , birds, reptiles* and also insects.

Clouded leopard

Coati

Coatis eat small animals and plants. They search for food on the ground with their long, sensitive noses. At night they sleep in the trees.

Bird-eating spider

Asian bird-eating spiders kill prey with a poisonous bite. They hunt insects, mice and even small birds.

*Mammals, Reptiles, 116.

Colors in the rain forest

All around the world, animals use their colors to blend into their background. They may also show off especially bright colors when they want to attract a mate, or to show they are frightened or angry. In rain forests, huge numbers of animals are brilliantly colored.

Bright colors

Many rain forest animals are brightly colored so they can be seen by other animals of the same kind. Other strikingly colored animals are able to blend in with the leafy background.

Different kinds of toucan have different bright colors on their beaks. They can easily recognize each other.

Toucan

Orchid mantis

Orchid mantises look like orchid flowers, so insects land on them. The mantises eat them.

Rhinoceros viper

Rhinoceros vipers from Africa have bright patterns but blend in with the leaves on the floor. Their poisonous bite paralyzes their prey.

Day geckos are very bright, but blend in with the leaves.

Day gecko

Attracting a mate

Many of the most dazzling birds in the world live in rain forests. The males are usually more stunning than the females. The males dance or show off special feathers to attract a mate.

Peacock

Indian male peacocks have long, brightly colored tail feathers which they spread out and shake.

Argus pheasants

Argus pheasants from Malaya and Borneo clear the ground and dance in a complicated pattern.

Bower birds build a special avenue, column or hut out of sticks. They decorate it with flowers, berries, snake skins, shells and man-made objects such as bottle tops and teaspoons. Sometimes they paint it with charcoal and saliva, using bark as a paintbrush, or plant moss gardens.

Bower bird

Color tricks

Chameleons can change the color of their skin to blend in with their background, to attract a mate, or when they are angry or frightened.

Count Raggi's bird of paradise

Chameleon

Chameleons change from white or yellow to green, brown or black when frightened or angry.

They catch insects in the hollow tip of their long sticky tongue which they flick out very quickly.

They have grasping toes and a strong tail for climbing and eyes that swivel to look in two different directions at once.

Warning colors

Many poisonous or nasty-tasting animals are brightly colored. When predators (hunters) have tasted one, they quickly learn to avoid animals with those bright colors. Other animals, which are not poisonous, are safe if they look like the poisonous ones, because predators avoid them too.

Grasshoppers warn other animals that they taste unpleasant with their bright colors.

Birds of paradise from Australia and New Guinea clear leaves off a patch of branches to let light shine onto their brilliant feathers. They bend over, spread out their feathers and clap their wings together.

Golden cock-of-the-rock cotinga

South American golden cock-of-the-rock cotingas hide their beak with bright feathers. They make a space on the ground and dance in front of the females.

Coral snakes are brightly colored to show that they are poisonous. Some harmless snakes are safe, too, because they look almost the same.

Harmless king snake

Poisonous coral snake

Living with people

As the number of people in the world gets bigger, more and more of the Earth's land surface is covered with towns and cities. This means that natural countryside habitats are lost. However, some plants and animals have learned to cope with life in towns, despite the people and the pollution, and even though there are no large open spaces.

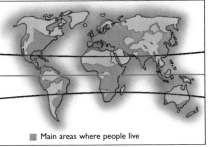

Main areas where people live

Finding food

Many animals living in towns or cities depend on people for their food.

Raccoon

Fox

Red foxes live in many European cities and raccoons in North American ones. At night they look through trash for food to eat.

Places to live

Many plants and animals live in warm buildings or on their walls. Others find small areas which are similar to their countryside habitat.

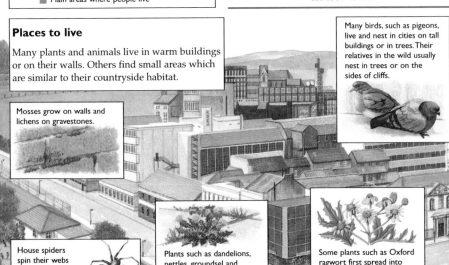

Mosses grow on walls and lichens on gravestones.

Many birds, such as pigeons, live and nest in cities on tall buildings or in trees. Their relatives in the wild usually nest in trees or on the sides of cliffs.

House spiders spin their webs on furniture and walls to catch small insects.

Plants such as dandelions, nettles, groundsel and goosegrass grow between sidewalks.

Some plants such as Oxford ragwort first spread into cities along railway lines. They often grow on trash dumps and waste land.

Many gulls find their food on trash dumps. They have changed their whole way of life to take advantage of this source of food.

Gull

Mice

Rats and mice live under floorboards and in sewers, coming out to scavenge for food left lying around. Sometimes there are more rats than people living in a city.

In the UK, blue tits have learned how to open milk bottles left outside people's doors, so that they can drink the milk.

Birds at a bird table

Blue tit

Many birds survive cold, hard winters, when the plants are covered in snow, because of food left out for them on bird tables.

Bats roost in attics and the tops of tall buildings. They come out at night to hunt insects.

Grassland plants grow in open grassy places such as yards and playing fields. Many kinds of insects live and feed on them. They are food for many birds and small animals.

Furniture beetles eat dead wood. They are just as at home in wooden furniture as in fallen logs.

House martins in the country build their nests on cliff ledges. In towns, they nest in the sheltered gap between roofs and walls.

Animals such as frogs live near rivers and ponds in parks and gardens.

People and parasites

Parasites are tiny living things that live on or inside other living things, called their hosts, and feed off them. Some kinds of parasites are harmless, but other kinds can cause diseases. Like many animals, people are host to many different kinds of parasites.

Feeding on others

The food that plants make and animals eat, gives them energy to live and grow. The energy-giving substances travel around inside them in liquids.

Plant sap contains these substances and in animals they are carried in blood and other body liquids. Many parasites feed on these liquids.

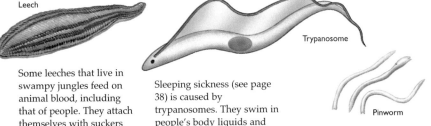

Leech

Trypanosome

Pinworm

Some leeches that live in swampy jungles feed on animal blood, including that of people. They attach themselves with suckers while they feed. When they are full, they drop off. They can survive for weeks on one meal.

Sleeping sickness (see page 38) is caused by trypanosomes. They swim in people's body liquids and soak up the food they need. People get them from other ill people via blood-sucking insects, such as tse-tse flies.

Pinworms are human parasites that live in the gut. They can grow to about 20mm (one inch) long. They eat bits of food.

Ticks, lice and fleas are insects that feed on blood. They have sucking mouths and claws to cling onto hairs or fur.

Fleas live on both rats and people. In the 1300s, a bacteria they carried spread to people. It caused a disease, called the Black Death. Millions of people died of the disease.

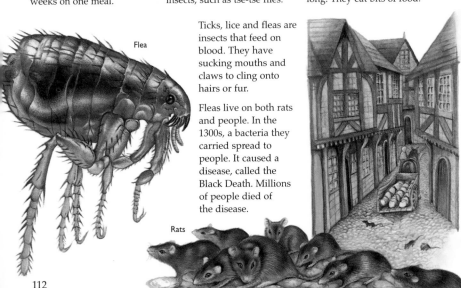

Flea

Rats

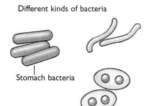

Bacteria and viruses

Bacteria and viruses are very tiny living things. Bacteria are made up of only one tiny cell*. Some live in or on other living things and feed off them.

Viruses are smaller than bacteria and can only live as parasites inside other cells. Some viruses, such as T4 bacteriophages, live inside bacteria.

Many kinds of harmless bacteria live off people. For example, thousands of tiny bacteria live in our stomachs. The bacteria feed by breaking up plant and animals material into simple substances. This helps us digest* our food.

Different kinds of bacteria

Stomach bacteria

These bacteria cause sore throats.

Other kinds of bacteria can cause diseases. They are called **germs**. Salmonella causes typhus and food poisoning. People need to eat ten million of them before they become ill.

Salmonella bacteria

Ten million salmonella bacteria fit in this space.

AIDS virus. It is actually 100 times smaller than one of the bacteria in human stomachs.

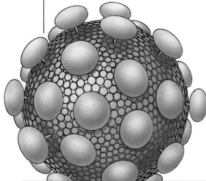

Different kinds of viruses

Tobacco mosaic virus

T4 Bacterio phage

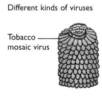

Viruses live inside plant and animal cells*. They cause diseases, such as colds, AIDS, rabies and chicken pox and are also germs. They attack cells by getting inside and taking over the nucleus (control center) of the cell. They make the cell make more new viruses.

The war against diseases

Animals, including people, all have defenses inside their bodies against diseases. The defenses are called the **immune system**.

The immune system is made up of cells* that can tell germs and body cells apart. They right off diseases by killing the germs that cause them.

An immune cell killing a cell that is not part of the body.

An immune cell kills a germ by "eating" it.

Immune cell

Germ

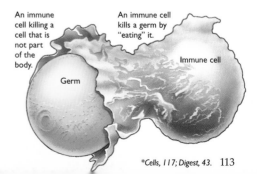

Endangered species

Scientists think that a million rare species of plants and animals may die out in the next 10 to 20 years. You can find out some reasons for this on pages 18-19. These species are called endangered species. The biggest threat is the destruction of wild areas when people cut down forests, make new farmland, let deserts spread, build cities, roads and mines and pollute areas.

Protecting plants

About 60,000 different kinds of plants, about a quarter of the total number of species in the world, are endangered.

Each kind of plant provides food or shelter for many different animals. If the plants become extinct, the animals that depend on them may be threatened.

Many mangrove swamps are destroyed for timber and to make room for farms and towns. The plants die and the animals lose their homes. In Malaysia, mangrove forests are cut down for timber. To protect them, they are cleared a bit at at time. Each area is then left alone for timber. To protect them, they are cleared a bit at a time. Each area is then left alone for 40 years. During this time the trees grow again and new ones are planted. The animals have plenty of forest left to live in.

Mangrove swamp

In places such as Canada, Brazil, Kenya and Australia, people are replanting trees where forests have been chopped down. It will take hundreds of years for the forests to grow back. However, as the new trees grow, many kinds of plants and animals may return that had been lost from these areas.

Young trees protected in tubes

Individual species of rare plants become endangered when people collect them. Golden barrel cacti and many kinds of slipper orchids are endangered because they are taken from the wild and sold.

Golden barrel cactus

Rothschild's slipper orchid

African violets are very rare in the wild, but are not likely to die out. This is because they are specially grown for sale, so collectors do not take them from the wild. They are now common as house plants, but will not become common again in the wild unless they are replanted.

African violet

Some rare plants are saved and stored in special botanic gardens, nurseries and reserves. The seeds are stored in seed banks. If the plants die out in the wild, they can be replanted from seeds from the saved plants. For example, in Wales, the last two tufted saxifrage plants were saved. New plants were grown from them and replanted in the wild.

Tufted saxifrage

Protecting animals

Thousands of rare species of animals are endangered because they are hunted, or because the plants that provide their food and homes are destroyed.

Many people now work to save them. There are many different ways that people can help rare animals.

Many animals are hunted for their skin or horns. However, governments have now made it illegal to sell skins of animals such as alligators, vicuñas and koalas, or items such as elephant tusks and turtle shells.

Alligator

Koala

Hawksbill turtle

Rhinoceroses are endangered because people kill them to sell their horns. In parts of Africa, people are protecting rhinoceroses by sawing off their horns, so that hunters leave them alone.

Rhinoceros with horns sawn off

The hunting of tigers was banned in 1970 and since then their numbers have more than doubled.

Tiger

Polar bears nearly died out because so many were killed for their skins and for sport. Many were also killed if they came near towns. To save them, many polar bears were moved away from towns and several countries agreed to protect them and the areas where they live. There are many more in the wild now.

Polar bear

Many butterflies, such as West African orange foresters, are endangered partly because people collect them, but also because so many wild areas where they used to live have been destroyed.

Orange forester

Many wild areas called reserves or national parks are being set aside. Here animals and plants are protected from people, but live in the wild.

Animals roam about in reserves

Spanish lynxes were endangered because so much of the forest they lived in had been cut down. However, they are now protected in a reserve in Coto Donana, Spain.

Spanish lynx

Some reserves are in special areas in the sea. In Florida there are areas where boats are not allowed to go, to protect manatees from being harmed by propellers.

Manatee

Whales such as humpbacks and blue whales were hunted so much in the past for meat and fat (made into oil), that they nearly died out. Although it is now illegal in most countries to hunt whales, people do still hunt them, or catch them accidentally in fishing nets.

Blue whale

Humpback whale

Sometimes where animals have very nearly died out, they are kept in special centers until their numbers have increased. They are put back in protected wild areas when there are enough of them to stand a good chance of surviving.

California condors died out in the wild because they are slow breeders*, their food is hard to find and people hunted them. However before they died out in the wild, some of their eggs were saved and hatched in special centers. The young birds were fed by hand-held puppets of adult condors, then released, but few survived.

Californian condor

Many golden lion tamarin monkeys have been bred in zoos and some have now been put back into a protected area of rainforest in Brazil. At first they live inside big cages in the forest so they learn to survive and find food in the wild while being protected from other animals.

Golden lion tamarins

*Slow breeders, 17.

Describing living things

To help them describe the living world, scientists have grouped together living things that are similar to each other. The biggest groups are called kingdoms. All the animals are in the animal kingdom and all the plants are in the plant kingdom. Inside these groups there are smaller groups, with even smaller ones inside them. The smallest groups of all are known as species*. The group names tell the scientists about the living things in them.

The plant kingdom

The main difference between plants and animals is that plants make their own food from sunlight, the gas called carbon dioxide and water, and they are called **autotrophs**.

Animals do not make food, but eat plants or other animals and are called **heterotrophs**.

Algae are simple plants. They may be tiny, such as phytoplankton*, or much larger, such as seaweed. They are often put with fungi in the group **thallophytes**.

Mosses are in a group called **bryophytes**. They have tiny root-like things (not true roots) which cling to surfaces rather than growing into the ground. They do not have xylem* and phloem* to carry water and food. They produce spores, like the ones produced by fungi (see page 65), in a case on a stalk. When the case opens, the spores blow away, land and grow into new plants.

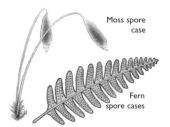

Moss spore case

Fern spore cases

Alga

Ferns also produce spores. The spore cases grow in groups under the leaves. Ferns have xylem and phloem and are in a group known as **pteridophytes**.

The animal kingdom

Scientists call the animals with a backbone in their body **vertebrates** and those without a backbone **invertebrates**. These are the two main groups in the animal kingdom. Both of these big groups contain other, smaller groups.

Vertebrates

There are about 45,000 different kinds of vertebrates living on Earth. They are divided into five main groups: fish, amphibians, reptiles, birds and mammals.

What is a fish?

Fish are cold-blooded* animals which live in water. They breathe using gills*, their bodies are covered with scales and they have fins. They lay many eggs in water.

What is an amphibian?

Newts, salamanders, frogs and toads are all **amphibians**. They are cold-blooded and spend some time on land, but lay their eggs in water. Their young breathe with gills, but the adults use lungs* on land and can breathe through their skins in air or water.

What is a reptile?

Turtles and tortoises, lizards, snakes and crocodiles are all **reptiles**. They are cold-blooded animals which live on land. They breathe air using lungs and have a dry, scaly skin. They lay their eggs on land.

What is a bird?

Birds are warm-blooded* animals. They have wings and their whole bodies are covered with feathers. They breathe air with lungs and produce young by laying eggs. They have beaks but no teeth.

What is a mammal?

Mammals are warm-blooded and have hair. They breathe air with lungs. The females feed their young with milk from their bodies. Two kinds of mammals, spiny anteaters and platypuses, lay eggs and are known as **monotremes**, but the rest produce live young. Some produce tiny live young and nurse them in a pouch. They are **marsupials**, and include kangaroos. All other mammals give birth to larger live young.

*Cold-blooded, 54; Gills, 86; Lungs, 80; Phloem, 14; Phytoplankton, 22; Species, 18; Warm-blooded, 54; Xylem, 14.

Plants such as conifers*, called **gymnosperms**, have xylem and phloem. Like flowering plants (see below) they grow new plants from seeds, formed when male **pollen** joins with female **ovules**. However, gymnosperms do not grow flowers, instead the pollen and ovules grow on **cones**. The seeds have no outer cases.

Cone   Flower

Flowering plants, such as palm trees, daffodils and roses, are called **angiosperms**. They have xylem and phloem and their pollen and ovules are made in flowers (see page 14). The pollen is carried to the ovules by wind, water or animals (see pages 34-35). Cases protect the seeds.

Other kingdoms

Almost all living things are made out of very tiny "building blocks" called **cells**, each of which has a control center called a **nucleus**. Some of the very tiniest living things have only one cell. They cannot really by called plants or animals, so many scientists put them in separate kingdoms.

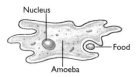

Nucleus

Food

Amoeba

Most tiny living things with one cell are put in a kingdom of their own called **protista**. Some, such as amoeba, take in food. Others make it from sunlight, like plants through photosynthesis*. Some can do both.

Bacteria* are often put in a kingdom called **monera**. They are tiny living things with only one cell. They are separated from the protista because the cell does not have a true nucleus.

Tiny bacteria on point of pin

Fungi are often put in a separate kingdom, the kingdom **fungi**. They are made up of very thin threads, but these are not made of cells. They get their food by taking in liquids from dead, rotting* plants and animals.

Fungi

Invertebrates

There are far more invertebrates than vertebrates living on Earth, about 950,000 different kinds. Some are so tiny that they can only be seen with a microscope. Others, such as giant squid, grow to 20 meters (65ft) long. The invertebrates are divided into many different groups.

Jellyfish, sea anemones and corals are put together in one group, called **coelenterates**, because they have soft, jelly-like bodies and catch prey with stinging tentacles.

Jellyfish   Starfish

Sea urchins and starfish are both in the same group, called **echinoderms** because they have tough, spiny skins and their bodies are made up of five identical parts.

Crabs, spiders, insects and centipedes are in a group called **arthropods**. Their bodies are divided into sections called **segments**, covered with a hard skin or shell. Their legs bend at joints. Spiders have eight legs and insects have six. There are more different kinds of insects in the world than any other animal.

Crab   Insect

Snails, oysters, mussels and octopuses have a soft body, with a hard shell either outside or inside their body. The group they are in is called **mollusks**.

Octopus

Earthworms and ragworms come from a group called **annelids**. Their bodies are made up of sections called **segments**, with an opening at each end.

Earthworm

Flatworm

Flatworms, such as tapeworms and liver flukes are put in a different group from earthworms, called **platyhelminthes.** They have only one opening in their body.

Sponge

Sponges are in a group of creatures called **porifera** which have stiff bodies. They filter feed* by passing water through holes in their bodies.

Glossary

Words that are explained in this glossary (pages 118-121) are printed in **bold type**.

Acid. A sour-tasting chemical. Plants and animals contain harmless weak acids. Some acids, however are dangerous.

Anthers. The male parts of flowers, where special male **cells** called pollen are made (see **pollination**, **fertilization**).

Aquatic. Living in water.

Arboreal. Living in trees.

Autotrophs. Living things that make their food. Plants make their food from sunlight, carbon dioxide and water. They are autotrophs.

Binary fission. The way that **cells** produce new cells as a plant or animals grows. First the nucleus and then the cell divides into two. This makes two new cells, the same size as the original one, each with a nucleus.

Parent cell

Nucleus

Nucleus splits in two

Two daughter cells

Cell begins to split

Biology. The scientific study of living things.

Blood. A liquid which is pumped around the bodies of animals, carrying oxygen, carbon dioxide and simple sugars and waste.

Blubber. A thick layer of fat under the skin of animals such as whales. It keeps them warm.

Botany. The scientific study of plants.

Bud. Part of a plant that grows into a flower or a leaf. Also, part of a cell or simple animal that splits off and grows to be exactly the same. This is called budding. For example, coral polyps produce buds (see page 28).

Camouflage. Skin, fur or feather colors which help an animal to blend in with its background.

Carnivore. A meat-eating animal.

Carpel. The word for the female part of a flower. It includes the **ovary**, together with its outer pieces, called the stigma and style. When **pollination** happens, the pollen first lands on the sticky stigma and then travels down the style to the ovary.

Cells. Very tiny "building blocks", each with a control center called a nucleus, from which almost all living things are made.

Chromosomes. Thread-like things in the nucleus of a **cell**, made of a complex chemical called DNA. Each is a chain of **genes**.

When a cell splits in two, its thread-like chromosomes wind up into sausage shapes.

This shows how the particles that make up DNA are arranged. They are in a spiral called a double helix.

Colony. A group made up of large numbers of one kind of plant or animal, living together. The word is most often used of insects, or sea birds such as gannets.

Community. A group of plants and animals living together in an **environment**, and dependent on each other in a **food web**.

Conservation. Protecting and preserving natural **environments**, so as to protect the plants and animals for the future.

Decomposer. An **organism** which causes dead plants to rot, by breaking them down into simple substances. Bacteria and fungi are decomposers.

Deforestation. The loss of trees from forested areas.

Demersal. Living on the bottom of the sea.

Desertification. The spread of deserts to new areas.

Detritus. Rotting bits of plant of animal material.

Digestion. The breakdown of food inside an animal's body into substances which the body can use to get energy and for growth.

Diurnal. A word describing plants with flowers that open and animals that are active, during daylight hours.

Dormant. A word describing a plant or animal that is resting for a time without growing, so using up very little energy or food.

Ecology. The study of the relationship between plants and animals and their **environment**.

Ecosystem. A community of plants and animals and their **environment**.

Embryo. A young plant inside a seed, or a young animal inside an egg or its mother's body. It is growing but not yet fully formed.

Endangered species. A species that many die out because of dangers such as a change of **environment**.

Endemic species. A species found only in a particular area. It is said to be endemic to that area.

Environment. The natural surroundings in which plants and animals live. Environments vary in different parts of the world depending on things such as how much sun and rain there is. Plants and animals living in deserts, tropical forests or polar regions become very good at living in their particular environments.

Epiphyte. A plant which grows on another plant for support, but does not harm it. For example, bromeliads grow on trees (see page 98).

Evolution. The changes which take place in animals and plants over millions of years. One of the ways in which scientists know about these changes is from studying **fossils** and comparing them to species of plants and animals that are alive today.

Extinct. A word describing a plant or animal species that has completely died out.

Fertilization. The joining together of special male and female **cells** to produce a new living thing. The female cells are eggs (see **ovary**) and the male ones are in pollen in flowers (see **pollination**) and **sperm** in animals.

Filter feeding. A way of feeding by sifting very tiny pieces of food out of water.

Fins. Parts which stick out from a fish's body and help it to swim. They are made from spines covered in skin.

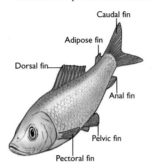

- Caudal fin
- Adipose fin
- Dorsal fin
- Anal fin
- Pelvic fin
- Pectoral fin

Flower. The part of a flowering plant which holds the male and female parts needed to produce seeds (see **anthers**, **ovary**). New young plants grow from the seeds.

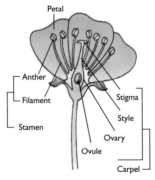

- Petal
- Anther
- Filament
- Stamen
- Stigma
- Style
- Ovary
- Ovule
- Carpel

Food web. A group of living things in a **community**, linked together by what they eat and what they are food for. There is a diagram of a North American forest food web on page 10.

Fossils. The hard parts of plants and animals preserved in rock over millions of years.

Genes. Chemical units that are joined together in chains to form the **chromosomes** of a living thing. Genes are the "codes" which say what a living thing is and what it looks like. For example, one gene may be the code for eye color, another for the code for sex (male or female).

Germination. The early growth of a seed or **spore**.

Herbivore. A plant-eating animal.

Heterotrophs. Living things which depend on plants or other animals to provide their food and cannot make their own. Animals are heterotrophs.

Hibernation. A sleep-like resting state which some kinds of animals go into during winter. Their body temperature drops when the conditions are cold and their bodies "slow down". This means they hardly use any energy, so they do not have to eat much.

Incubate. To keep eggs warm until the young hatch out.

Larvae. Young forms that look very different from the adults, but which gradually change to look like them.

Littoral. Living on the sea shore, or near it in shallow water, or living on the bottom of a lake near the shore.

Metamorphosis. The changes a **larva** goes through before it turns into an adult.

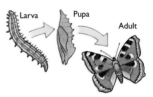

- Larva
- Pupa
- Adult

Microbiology. The study of living things so tiny that they can only be seen through a microscope.

Migration. Regular long journeys made by animals, for example, moving in winter to places where there is more food and then coming back in the summer.

Mimic. An animal or plant that looks or sounds similar to another. Many gain extra protection from being mimics, because they mimic a poisonous species and so other animals avoid them.

Insect mimicking leaf

Minerals. Certain kinds of substances found in the ground and in the bodies of all living things. Plants take minerals from the ground to help them grow.

Nocturnal. Active at night.

Nutrients. Food substances that plants and animals can break down so they can grow or get energy.

Nymph. A young insect form that looks like the adult, but is smaller and has no wings. Locust hoppers (see page 56) are nymphs.

Omnivore. An animal that eats both plants and other animals.

Organism. A living thing.

Ovary. The female part of a flower and the part in a female animal where eggs are made. The eggs are special **cells**, called ovules in flowers and ova in animals (see also **fertilization**).

Parasite. A plant or animal which lives on or in another plant or animal, called its host, and gets all its food from it. The host may or may not be harmed.

Pelagic. Living in the open water of a sea or lake.

Petals. Leaf-like parts of a flower, often colorful to attract insects to **pollinate** the flower.

Pollination. The carrying of male cells called pollen from the **anther** of a flower to an **ovary** (see **fertilization**).

Pollutant. A poisonous substance that harms the **environment**.

Predator. An animal that hunts and kills other animals for food.

Prey. An animal that is hunted by another animal for food. A bird of prey is one that hunts other animals, which are its prey.

Pupa. A stage during the **metamorphosis** of some insect **larvae**. The larva stops moving and feeding and, inside a case, changes into the adult form.

Radiation. A term describing many different kinds of energy. Some kinds are harmless, such as light, heat and sound. Other kinds can be dangerous, such as ultra-violet radiation and radiation from nuclear waste.

Recycling. The return of natural substances to soil, air or water and their reuse by living things.

Reproduction. The production, by adult living things, of new young living things.

Saprophyte. A living thing that feeds on rotting plant or animal material. For example, some fungi are saprophytes.

Scavenger. An animal which does not hunt or kill, but eats dead animals, for example, the animals which **predators** have killed.

Scrub. An area of land where most of the plants are small bushes and there are hardly any tall trees.

Soil. A mixture of tiny particles of rock and rotting plant and animal material, with water and air between them.

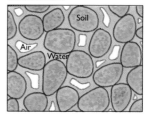

Sperm. The special cells made by a male animal which come together with female cells to produce new life (see **fertilization**).

Spore. Tiny particles produced by some fungi and simple plants. They grow into new plants.

Stamens. The word for a male part of a flower - an **anther** - together with the stalk that supports it, called a filament.

Symbiont. A plant or animal living with another plant or animal, each being useful to the other. For example, hermit crabs and sea anemones have a sybiotic relationship (see page 29).

Terrestrial. Living on land

Territory. An area where an animal or animals live. Animals defend their territory against intruders, especially animals of the same kind.

Zoology. The scientific study of animals.

Index

Where a page number is in **bold type**, this means it is the main entry for this word.

A

aardvark, 49
aardwolf, 49
acacia, 38, 41
acid, 67, **118**
acid rain, **67**, 87
addax antelope, 55
African violet, 114
AIDS, 113
albatross, wandering, 35
alder, 60
alga, algae, 4, 61, 74, 87, **116**, 117
alligator, 18, 89, 114
alpine cough, 83
alpine marmot, 78
Alps, 78
Amazon river, 94-95
ammonite, 4
amoeba, 117
amphibians, 5, 80, 88-89, 116
anaconda, 95
anchovy, 23
angiosperm, 117
angler fish, 26
animal kingdom, 116-117
annelid, 117
annual rings, 15
ant, 38, 49, 51, 100
　army, 101
　leaf cutter, 100
Antarctica, 72, 73, **74-75**
anteater, 49
　spiny, 100, 116
antelope, 42, 46
　addax, 55
　pronghorn, 46
　saiga, 46
　Thompson's gazelle, 47
　wildebeest, 39, 42, 43
anthers, 14, 70, **118**
antlers, 16, 61, 69
ape, 5, 104-105
aphid, 62
apple, 14
aquatic, 118
arapaima, 94
arboreal, 70, 118
archer fish, 33
Arctic, 6, 9, 11, 20, 58, 72-73, **76-77**
arctic fox, 11, 73

arctic hare, 77
arctic ringlet, 76
Argus pheasant, 108
armadillo, nine-banded, 47
armored catfish, 87
army ant, 101
arrow poison frog, 95
arrowhead, 84
arthropods, 117
ash, mountain, 70
ass, wild, 55
autotrophs, 116, 118
aye aye, 101

B

babies
　mammals, 16
　marsupial, 5
baboon, 39
bacteria, 13, 27, 30, 65, **113**, 117
badger, European, 59
baleen whales, 23
banana, 99
banded (cleaner) shrimp, 29
bandicoot, rabbit, 71
baobab, 38, 41
barbel, 84
barbirusa, 97
barbs, 92
barbules, 92
bark, 15
barnacles, 22, 28
barrel cactus, golden, 114
bat, 7, 111
　fish-eating, 95
　fruit, 97
　pipistrelle, 7
　vampire, 107
beaks, 31, 35, 37, 45, 69, 71, 92, 93, 95, 108, 116
bear, 10, 64
　polar, 6, 77, 115
　spectacled, 83
　sun, 101
beaver, 48, 67, 90
beech, 8, 59
beech roller moth, 62
bees, 6
beetle, 38, 51, 62, 64, 76
　furniture, 111
　Namib, 53
　stag, 7
　whirligig, 86
　wood-tunnelling, 70

biology, 118
birch, 60
bird of paradise, 109
bird-eating spider, 107
birds, 80, 116
　attracting a mate, 63, 93, **108-9**
　endangered, 19
　flightless, 37, 47
　sea/water, 21, 31, 35, 92-93
bison, 42
Black Death, 112
black grouse, 79
black rhino, 42
black-bellied hamster, 48
bladders (seaweed), 31
blood, 80, 112, 118
bloodwood, 70
blubber, 73, **118**
blue heron, 92
blue tit, 111
blue whale, 23, 115
blue-footed booby, 35
boar, wild, 65
bobcat, 10
booby, blue-footed, 35
botany, 118
bower bird, 108
box, 70
brain coral, 28
bream, 88
breathing, 7, 12, 23, 27, 80-81, 86, 95
breeding, 16, 17
bromeliads, 98
browsers, 42
bryophytes, 116
budgerigar, 52
buds, 8, 28, **118**
buffalo, 79
burdock, 35
burrowing owl, 48
bushbaby, 103
butterfly, 17, 19, 61-63, 76, 97, 115
　arctic ringlet, 76
　orange forester, 115
　purple emperor butterfly, 7
　swallowtail butterfly, 19
butterfly fish, 28

C

cacao tree, 99
cactus, 6, 19, 50, 53
　golden barrel, 110
　saguaro, 53
caiman, 95

camels, 5, 52, 55
camouflage, **118**
    big cats, 106
    chameleon, 109
    grassland animals, 4
    octopus, 27
    okapi, 103
    plaice, 24
    tapir, 91
    tundra animals, 77
    woodcock, 64
canopy, **60**, 62-63, 70, 96-97, 102-103
capercaille, 68
capybara, 94
carbon cycle, 12
caribou (reindeer), 9, 73, 76, 77
carnivores, 44, **118**
carpel, 118, 119
carpet snake, 71
caterpillar, 62
catfish, armored, 87
cats, 16, 51, 106-107
cells, 113, **117**, 118
centipedes, 64, 117
    giant, 100
century plant, 57
CFCs, 75
chameleon, 109
chamois, 78, 82
cheetah, 44
chestnut, Moreton Bay, 19
chewing the cud, 43
chimpanzee, 105
chipmunk, 69
chough, alpine, 83
Christmas-tree worm, 28
chromosome, 118
chrysalis, 63
cichlid, 88
clams, giant, 28
cleaner (banded) shrimp, 29
cleaner wrasse, 29
clouded leopard, 107
coal, 36
coati, 107
cockle, 30
cock-of-the-rock cotinga, golden,
    109
coconut, 34
cold, coping with the, 58, 72, 73,
    80-81
cold-blooded animals, **54**, 97, 116
coelenterates, 117
colobus monkey, 105
colonies, **49**, 118
color, 27, 77, 95, 108-109

colugo, 103
community, 10, 11, 18, **118**
condor, Californian, 115
cones, 66, 117
conifers, 66-69, 117
conservation, 118
constrictors, 45
consumers, 10-11
continental shelf, 21
coral, 4, 117
    brain, 28
    elkhorn, 28
    polyps, 28, 29
    reefs, 21, 28, 29
    sea fan, 28
coral snake, 109
cord grass, 32
cotinga, golden cock-of-the-rock,
    109
courtship, 93, 108-109
coyote, 46, 53
coypu, 91
crab, 20, 30, 117
    fiddler, 33
    furrowed, 30
    hermit, 29
    robber, 36
crane, 93
crested grebe, great, 93
crinoid, 4
crocodile, 116
crossbill, 69, 79
crowfoot, water, 84, 88
crown of thorns starfish, 28
curlew, 31
cypress, 15

D

daisy, 14
dam (beaver), 90
damsel fish, 25
dandelion, 110
date palm, 51
day gecko, 108
death puffer fish, 29
deciduous trees, 8, 58-59, 60-61, 79
decomposers, 118
deer, 16, 61
demersal, 118
desert shrimp, 57
desertification, 118
deserts, 6, 9, 50-57
    frozen, 72

desman, 83
detritus, 118
digestion, 43
dik dik, 42
dinosaurs, 5, 18
dipper, 87
diseases, 112-113
diurnal, 118
divers, 76
dog whelks, 31
dogs, 16
    hunting, 44
    prairie, 48
    wild, 79
dolphins, 23, 94
dominant species, 58, 60
dormant, 118
dormice, 8
douroucouli, 105
dragonfly, Emperor, 85
drip tip, 96
duck-billed platypus, 5, 90, 116
duckweed, 85
dugong, 33
dust bowl, 57

E

eagle, **44**, 68
    golden, 68, 78
    harpy, 107
    Philippine, 19, 97
ears
    bat, 7
    fennec fox, 54
    jackrabbit, 55
    okapi, 103
    polar animals, 73
earthworm, 64, 117
echinoderm, 117
ecology, 118
ecosystem, 118
eel, 22, 23
    electric, 94
    gulper, 26
    moray, 29
eel grass, 32
eggs, **16-17**, 22, 28, 32, 49, 55-56, 62,
    74-76, 81, **88-89**, 90, 93, 115-116
eland, 19
electric eel, 94
elephants, 18, 39, 42, 47, 79, 97, 114
elk, see moose
elkhorn, coral, 28
elver, 22

embryo, 119
emerald tree boa, 102
endangered species, 17, 18-19, 69, 83, 114-115, 119
endemic species, 36, 119
environments, 6-7, 119
  preservation of, 19
epiphyte, 119
estuaries, 30, 32-33
eucalyptus, 41, 70
evergreen trees, 9, 58, 59, 60, 66-67, 70, 79, 96
evolution, 119
extinction, 4, 18-19, 99, 119
eyes/eyesight, 7, 24, 27, 44, 46, 103, 105, 106

F

falcon, 50
  peregrine, 69
fan worm, 28
farming/farmers, 13, 41, 57
fast breeders, 17
feathers, 31, 50, 55, 64, 73, 74, 80, **92**
fennec fox, 54
fern, 61, 116
  tree, 36
fertilization, 16, 88, 119
fertilizers, 87
fiddler crab, 33
fig, 35
  strangler, 98
filter feeding, 22, 23, 28, 117, 119
finches, Galapagos, 37
fins, 24, 119
fireweed, 73
fir trees, 9, 58, 66
fish, 5, 24-27, 32, 84, 86, 88-89, 116
  angler fish, 26
  arapaima, 94
  archer fish, 33
  armored catfish, 87
  barbel, 84
  bream, 88
  butterfly, 28
  cichlid, 88
  cleaner wrasse, 29
  damsel, 25
  death puffer, 29
  flying fish, 24
  four-eyed, 33
  grayling, 84
  great white shark, 24

hatchet, 26
lamprey, 89
lungfish, 87
minnow, 8
mudskipper, 33
paddlefish, 88
pearl, 29
pike, 89
piranha, 95
plaice, 24
puffer, 29
ray, 25
remora, 25
sail, 25
salmon, 32, 84
shark, 24, 25
  surgeon, 29
  tench, 84
  tripod fish 27
  viper, 26
  whale shark, 23
fish-eating bat, 95
flamingo, 93
flat fish, 24, 25
flea, 112
flightless birds, 37, 47
flowers, 119
  and insects, 6
  and pollination, 14
  desert, 57
  rainforest, 99
flukes, liver, 117
fly, 56, 62
  pine saw, 66
  tse-tse, 38, 112
flying fish, 24
flying frog, 103
flying lizard, 103
flying squirrel, 63
flytrap, Venus, 91
food chain, 10, 11
food, finding, 7, 31, 37, 68-69, 82, 83, 92, 110-111
food webs, 10, 119
forest hog, 79
forests,
  deciduous, 60-65, 79
  evergreen, 66-71, 79
  temperate, 58-71
fossa, 36
fossil fuels, 12
fossil, 4, 5, 36, 119
four-eyed fish, 33
fox, 7, 51, 52, 69, 77
  arctic, 11, 73
  fennec, 54

  red, 79, 110
foxglove, 14
fresh water, 32, 84-95
freshwater stingray, 95
frigate bird, 35
frog, 17, 86, 87, 98, 111, 116
  arrow poison, 95
  flying, 103
  tree, 103
fruit bat, 97
fruits, 60, 99
fungus/fungi, 65, 66, 74, 100, 117
fur, 54, 69, 77, 91, 102
furniture beetle, 111
furrowed crab, 30

G

gazelle, Thompson's, 47
gecko, 7
  day, 108
  Seychelles, 36
gene, 119
gentian, 81
gerbil, 53
gerenuk, 42
germination, 14
germs, 113
giant centipede, 101
giant clam, 28
giant kelp, 31
giant panda, 19
giant squid, 26, 177
giant tortoise, 19
giant tube worm, 27
gibbon, 104
gill rakers, 23
gills, 23, 28, 86, 87, 116
giraffe, 42, 47
global warming, 12
goat, Rocky Mountain, 82
golden barrel cactus, 114
golden cock-of-the-rock cotinga, 109
golden eagle, 68, 78
golden lion tamarin, 115
goose, greylag, 69
goosegrass, 110
gorilla, 18, 104
  mountain, 83
goshawk, 10
grasses, 14, 32, 38, **40-41**, 81, 98
  cord, 32
  eel, 32
  pampas, 41

grasshoppers, 38, 109
  desert, see locust
grasslands, 38-49
grayling, 84
grazers, 42-43
great crested grebe, 93
great grey owl, 67
great white shark, 24
grebe, great crested, 93
greenhouse effect, 12
grey kangaroo, 71
grey owl, great, 67
greylag goose, 69
grooming, 105
groundsel, 110
grouse
  black, 79
  sage, 47
  sand, 51
  spruce, 66
grubs, 62
  wood-tunnelling, 62, 63
guava, 99
gull, 72, 111
gulper eel, 26
gum tree, 70
  scribbly gum, 70
gymnosperm, 117

H

hamster, black-bellied, 48
hare, 67, 77
  arctic, 77
  Patagonian, see mara
harpy eagle, 107
hatchet fish, 26
hawksbill, turtle, 114
hawthorn, 60
hazel 59
heart, 80
hedgehog, 64
hemlock, 66
herbivores, 42-43, 46, 119
herds, 9, 39, 46, 82
hermit crab, 29
heron, 92
heterotrophs, 119
hibernation, 8, 59, 78, 119
hippo, 42, 43
hog, forest, 79
holly, 60
honey possum, 70
honeysuckle, 7
hornbill, 97

hornwort, 88
horse, 16
house martin, 111
house spider, 110
howler monkey, 103
humpback whale, 115
humming bird, 80
hunting dog, 44
hyena, 45

I

ibex, 82
ibis, scarlet, 95
ichneumon wasp, 62
immune system, 113
indri lemur, 37
insects, 5, 51, 53, 56, 60, **62-63**, 73,
  76, 78, 85, 86, 100-101, 117
  and pollination, 14
  colonies, 49
invertebrates, 116, 117
ironbark, 70
islands, 34-37

J

jacana, 92
jackrabbit, 55
jaguar, 107
jay, 61
jellyfish, 4, 23, 117

K

kakapo, 37
kangaroo, 46, 116
  grey, 71
  red, 46
  tree, 5
kangaroo rat, 51
kelp, giant, 31
killer whale, 20
king snake, 109
kingdoms, 116-117
kingfisher, 85, 92
kinkajou, 102
kiwi, 37
knot, 31
koala, 70, 114
komodo dragon, 36
kookaburra, 71
krill, 23
kudu, 42

L

lakes, 73, 84-93
lammergeier, 81
lamprey, 89
large ground finch, 37
larvae, 17, 62, 84, 85, 86, 119
lateral lines, 25
leaf cutter ant, 100
leaf litter, 60, 64, 100
leaf miner, 63
leatherback turtle, 23
leech, 112
lemming, 11, 67, 73, 77
lemur,
  indri, 37
  lesser mouse, 37
leopard, 44, 79, 106
  clouded, 107
  snow, 83
leopard seal, 72, 73
lesser mouse lemur, 37
lettuce, sea, 31
liana, 98
lice, 112
lichen, 30, 61, 66, 74, 78, 80, 110
lily trotter, 92
lion, 39, 44
littoral, 119
liver fluke, 117
lizard, 7, 51, 54, 116
  flying lizard, 103
  gecko, 7, 36, 108
  komodo dragon, 36
  stumpy-tailed (shingle-back), 53
llama, 5, 81
lobelia, 79
lobster, 20, 27
locust, 51, 56, 62
long-tailed tit, 63
loris, slow, 104
lungfish, 87
lungs, 80, 87, 116
lynx, 67
  Spanish, 115

M

malchite sunbird, 79
malee fowl, 55
mammals, 80, 116
  babies/young, 16-17
  swimming, 90-91
mammoth, woolly, 18

manatee, 33, 115
mandrill, 104
mango, 99
mangrove swamps, 33, 114
manta ray, 25
mantis, 101
 orchid, 108
maple, 59, 60
mara, 48
marabou stork, 39
marmoset, 105
marmot, alpine, 78
marsupial mice, 54
marsupials, 5, 70, 91, 116
marten, pine, 68, 79
martin, house, 111
matamata turtle, 94
mate, attracting a, 93, 105, 108-109
mating, 16
meat-eating animals see carnivore
meat-eating plants, 91
meerkat, 38, 48
mesquite bush, 52
metamorphosis, 63, 119
microbiology, 120
midwife toad, 89
migration, 9, 42, 59, 73, 120
milfoil, spiked water, 88
millipede, 64
 pill, 100
mimic, 120
minerals, 21
mink, 69
minnow, 84
moa, 37
mole, 64
mole rat, naked, 49
mollusks, 117
monkey, 79, 104-105
 colobus monkey, 105
 douroucouli, 105
 golden lion tamarin, 115
 howler monkey, 103
 mandrill, 104
 proboscis monkey, 33
 spider monkey, 19, 104
 squirrel monkey, 104
 uakari, 104
monotremes, 116
moose, 67, 69
moray eel, 29
Moreton Bay chestnut, 19
mosquito, 76, 86
moss, 61, 66, 73, 74, 78, 110, 116
moss campion, 73
moth, 7, 51, 56, 62

beech roller, 62
 privet hawk, 7
mountain ash, 70
mountain gorilla, 83
mountains, 78-83
 underwater, 21
mouse, 16, 17, 111
 marsupial mouse, 54
 woodmouse, 60
mud flats, 30, 32
mudskipper, 33
mushroom, 65
musk oxen, 76, 77
muskrat, 69
mussel, 30, 117

N

naked mole rat, 49
Namib beetle, 53
nectar, 6, 14, 70, 91
needles (leaves), 9, 66, 67
nests, 49, 61, 89, 110, 111
nettle, 110
newt, 89, 116
nightingale, 60
nitrates, 13, 21, 87, 91
nitrogen, 13
nitrogen cycle, 13
nocturnal animals, 7
Norway spruce, 66
nucleus, 113, 117
numbat, 70
nutrients, 120
nymph, 120

O

oak, 8, 15, 59, 60-61
oases, 51
oceans, 20-33, 72
ocelot, 107
ocotillo, 53
octopus, 26-27, 117
oil pollution, 31
okapi, 103
omnivores, 64, 120
opposum, 65
 water, 91
orange forester, 115
orangutan, 96
orchid, 34, 96, 98, 114
orchid mantis, 108
organism, 120
ostrich, 47

otter, 90
ovary, 14, 118, 120
ovules, 14, 117
owl, 50, 61
 burrowing, 48
 great grey, 67
oxen, musk, 76, 77
Oxford ragwort, 110
oyster, 117
oystercatcher, 31
ozone, 75

P

packs, 44, 76
paddlefish, 88
palm tree, 34 ,98
 date, 51
pampas grass, 41
panda, giant, 19
pangolin, 100
pansy, 15
papaya, 99
paradise, bird of, 109
parasites, 98, **112-113**, 120
parrot,
 kakapo, 37
 red-capped, 71
passion fruit, 99
Patagonian hare, see mara
peacock, 108
pearl fish, 29
peccary, 55
pelagic, 120
pelican, 92
penguin, 72, 74-75
 Emperor, 74-75
people, 12, 13, 18, 19, 37, 47, 57, 59,
 101, **110-113**, 114-115
peppermint, 70
peregrine falcon, 69
periwinkle, rosy, 99
permafrost, 73
petals, 120
petrel, 74, 75
phalangid, spider, 78
pheasant, Argus, 108
Philippine eagle, 19, 97
phloem, 14, 15, 116, 117
phosphates, 21
photosynthesis, 7, 21, 22, 31
phytoplankton, 22, 116
pigeon, 110
pika, 83
pike, 89

pill millipede, 100
pine marten, 68, 79
pine saw fly, 66
pine trees, 9, 58, 66
pinworms, 112
pipistrelle bat, 7
piranha, 95
pit viper, Wagler's, 97
pitcher plant, 91
plaice, 24
plankton, 20, 21, 22, 72, 74, 88
plant kingdom, 116-117
plant-eating animals, see herbivore
plants, **14-15, 40-41, 98-99**
  endangered, 19, 114
  growth of, 13, **15**
  making food, 7, 10
  meat-eating, 91
  plant year, 8
platyhelminthes, 117
platypus, duck-billed, 5, 90, 116
plover, 73
poison/poisonous animals, 95, 109
  amphibian, 95
  fish, 29, 95
  invertebrates, 57, 64
  mammals, 90, 91
polar bear, 6, 77, 115
polar regions, 58, **72-77**
pollen, 14, 15
pollination, 14, 56, 88, 120
pollutant, 120
pollution, 13, 17, 30, 31, 67, 87
polyps, coral, 28
pond skater, 85
poppy, 15
porcupine, 68
porifera, 117
Portuguese man o'war, 23
possum, honey, 70
potto, 102
prairie dog, 48
prairie rattlesnake, 48
prairies, 42
predators, 44, 120
prehensile tail, 102
prey, 44, 120
prides, 44
primates, 104
primrose, 7
privet hawk moth, 7
proboscis monkey, 33
producers, 10, 11
pronghorn antelope, 46
prop roots, 33
ptarmigan, 73

pteridophytes, 116
puff adder, 45
puffer fish, 29
puffin, 35
puma, 83
pupa, 63
purple emperor butterfly, 7
python, 45

Q

queen (insect), 49

R

rabbit, 10, 46
raccoon, 65, 110
radiation, ultra-violet, 75, 120
rafflesia, 98
ragworm, 32, 117
ragwort, Oxford, 110
rainforest, **96-109**
rare animals, 19, 83, 114-115
rat, 16, 48, 111-112
  kangaroo, 51
rattle, 48
rattlesnake, prairie, 48
ray, manta, 25
recycling, 120
red-capped parrot, 71
red fox, 79, 110
red kangaroo, 46
reefs, 21, **28-29**
reindeer, see caribou
reindeer moss, 73
remora, 25
reproduction, 14, 16
reptiles, 116
rhea, 46, 47
rhinoceros, 17, 47, 79, 114
  black, 42
  white, 43
rhinoceros viper, 108
rhodedendron, 60
ringlet, arctic, 76
river dolphin, 94
rivers, 20, 21, 32, 84-95
roadrunner, 53, 54
robber crab, 36
Rocky Mountain goat, 82
rodents, **48**, 53, 94
roots, 14, 32, 33, 40, 52, 81
  buttress, 96
  prop, 33

rose, wild, 14
roseate spoonbill, 93
rosy periwinkle, 99
rotting, 4, 12, 13, 21, 64, **65**, 66, 91, 100
rubber tree, 99
rushes, 61

S

sable, 69
sage grouse, 47
saguaro cactus, 53
saiga antelope, 46
sail fish, 25
salamander, 81, 116
salmon, 32, 84
salmonella, 113
sand dunes, 50, 51
sand grouse, 51
sap, 62, 112
saprophyte, 120
savannah, 38, 44
saxifrage, tufted, 114
scarlet ibis, 95
scavengers, 44, 45, 72, 77, 111, 120
scorpion, 57
scribbly gum, 70
scrub, 120
sea anemone, 6, 29, 117
sea aster, 32
sea birds, 21, 34, 35, 74
sea cow, 33
sea cucumber, 29
sea fan, 28
sea horse, 28
sea lettuce, 31
sea lion,
sea shore, 6, **30-31**
sea snake, 23
sea spider, 27
sea urchin, 28, 117
seal, 34, 72-76
  elephant, 75
  leopard, 72, 73
seas, 20-25
  coral reefs, 28-29
  polar, 72
  shore, 6, **30-31**
seasons, 6, **8-9**, 38, 42, 58, 68, 72-73, 96
seaweed, 31, 116
secretary bird, 45
seeds, 34-35, 41, 117
  conifer, 66
  deciduous tree, 60
  desert plants, 9, 56, 57

mountain grass, 81
of endangered species, 114
reproduction, 14
serval, 39
Seychelles gecko, 36
shark, 24, 25
great white, 24
whale, 23
shell, spire, 32
shelled animals, 4, 22, 30, 32
shield bug, 62
shoals, 25
shoebill, 93
shore birds, 31
shoreline, sea, 30-31
shrew, 10, 67
water, 91
shrike, 53
shrimp, 26, 32
banded (cleaner), 29
desert, 56-57
shrub layer, 60
silt, 32, 84, 94
skimmer, 92
skua, 72
skunk, 65, 59
sleeping sickness, 38, 112
slipper orchid, Rothschild's 114
sloth, 102
slow breeders, 17, 18, 115
slow loris, 104
slug, 64
smell, sense of, 25, 37, 106
snail, 64, 117
snake, 45, 48, 116
anaconda, 95
carpet, 71
coral, 109
emerald tree boa, 102
king, 109
prairie rattlesnake, 48
puff adder, 45
python, 45
rhinoceros viper, 108
sea, 23
Wagler's pit viper, 97
snow leopard, 83
soil, 13, 66, 67, 120
spadefoot toad, 56
Spanish lynx, 115
sparrowhawk, 69
species, 17, 18-19, 36-37, 116
dominant, 60
endangered, 17, 18-19,
114-115
spectacled bear, 83

sperm, 16, 88, 120
sperm whale, 27
spider, 64, 78, 117
bird-eating, 107
house, 110
phalangid, 78
sea, 27
tarantula, 57
water, 86
spider monkey, 19, 104
spiked water milfoil, 88
spiny anteater, 100
spire shell, 32
splendid wren, 71
sponges, 28, 117
spoonbill, roseate, 93
spores, 65, 116, 120
springtail, 81
spruce, 58, 66
spruce grouse, 66
squid, 20, 26-27
giant, 26-27
squirrel, 48, 60, 66, 77
flying, 63
squirrel monkey, 104
stag beetle, 7
stalking, 44
stamen, 70, 120
starfish, 22, 30, 31, 117
crown of thorns, 28
Steller's sea cow, 33
steppes, 46, 48
stingray, freshwater, 95
stoat, 77
stomach, 43, 113
stonefly, 84
stork, marabou, 39
strangler fig, 98
stringy bark, 70
stumpy-tailed (shingle-back)
lizard, 53
succession, 11
suckers,
remora, 25
squid, 26
tarsier, 102
sun bear, 101
sunbird, malachite, 79
sundew, 91
sunflower, 15
sungold, 57
surgeon fish, 29
Surinam toad, 89
swallow, 9
swallowtail butterfly, 19
swamps, mangrove, 22, 114

swan, 76
sweating, 54
swim bladder, 24
sycamore, 60
symbiont, 120

T

tadpole, 17, 86, 87
tail, prehensile, 102
takahe, 37
tapeworm, 117
tapir, 91
tarantula, 57
tarsier, 102
tartaruga, 89
tasmanian devil, 70, 71
tayra, 107
teeth, 25, 27, 43, 89, 95
temperate, 8, 15, 38, 58-71, 78-79,
84-85
temperature, 50, 54-55
tench, 84
tentacles, 6, 23, 26, 117
termites, 38, 49, 101
terrestrial, 120
territory, 63, 68, 120
thallophytes, 116
thistle, 34
Thompson's gazelle, 47
thorn bushes, 41
threatened/endangered species,
17, **18-19**, 69, **114-115**
thrift, 32
thylacine, 37
ticks, 112
tides, 6, 30, 32
tiger, 18, 106, 115
timberline, 78, 82
tit,
blue, 111
long-tailed, 63
toad, 56, 116
midwife, 89
spadefoot, 56
Surinam, 89
toadstool, 65
toothed whales, 23, 27
torpor, 80
tortoise, 116
giant, 19
toucan, 108
tree fern, 36
tree frog, 103
tree kangaroo, 5

trees,
   deciduous, 8, 58, 59, 79
   evergreen, 9, 58, 66-67, 79
   farming of, 59, 110
   grassland, 40-41
   growth of, 15, 40
   rainforest, 96-99
   temperate forest, 58-59, 60, 66
tripod fish, 27
tropics, 8, 15, 21, 38, 59
   mountain, 79
   rain forest, 96-97
trypanosomes, 112
tse-tse fly, 38, 112
tuatara, 36
tube worm, giant, 27
tufted saxifrage, 114
tundra, 73, 76
tunnels, 48
turtle, 23, 114, 116
   hawksbill, 114
   leatherback, 23
   matamata, 94
tusks, 76, 114

U

uakari, 104
ultra-violet radiation, 75

V

vampire bat, 107
vegetarian tree finch, 37
venom, 45
Venus flytrap, 91
vertebrates, 116
vicuña, 5, 82, 114
violet, African, 114
viper,
   rhinoceros, 108
   Wagler's pit, 97
viper fish, 26

vireo, 10
viruses, 113
volcanoes, 34
voles, 10, 67
   water, 85
vulture, 39, 45
   white-backed, 45
   white-headed, 45

W

waders/wading birds, 31, 76
wallaby, 70, 71
wallcreeper, 81
walrus, 76
warbler finch, 37
warm-blooded animals, **54-55**, 116
wasp, ichneumon, 62
water birds, 31, 76, **92-93**
water crowfoot, 84, 88
water cycle, 20, 84
water lily, 88
water milfoil, spiked, 88
water opossum, 91
water shrew, 91
water spider, 86
water vapor, 20, 40
water vole, 85
waterhole, 52
webbed feet, 90, 91
weevil, 60
welwitschia, 52
whale, 17, 18, 23
   blue, 23, 115
   humpback, 115
   killer, 20
   sperm, 27
whale shark, 23
whelk, dog, 31
whirligig beetle, 86
wild ass, 55
wild boar, 65
wild dog, 79

wild rose, 14
wildebeest, 39, 42, 43
willow, 61
wilt, 40
wolf, 76, 77
wolverine, 68
wombat, 5
wood sorrel, 6
woodcock, 64
woodlice, 64
woodmouse, 60
woodpecker, 63
woodpecker finch, 37
wood-tunnelling beetle, 70
wood-tunnelling grub, 62, 63
woolly mammoth, 18
worm, 20, 21, 30, 117
   Christmas-tree worm, 28
   earthworm, 64
   fan, 28
   giant tube, 27
   pinworm, 112
   ragworm, 32
   tapeworm, 117
wren, 60
   splendid, 71

X

xylem, 14, 15, 116, 117

Y

yak, 80
young, 8, 11, **16-17, 56**, 58, **62**, 116

Z

zebra, 39, 42, 43
zoology, 120
zooplankton, 22